Philosophers on God is brilliantly readable, and the topic is endlessly fascinating. Whether God exists or not, He or She has many advantages for the philosopher as a topic of speculation, not least that we are not likely to run out of things to say about the matter, because it will never be resolved. In this well-structured book, Jack Symes faces several eminent thinkers, some believers and some not, with exactly the sort of questions we'd put forward ourselves if we could think clearly enough. Some of their answers are more familiar than others, naturally; some surprised me; all told me something, and some told me a lot; none persuaded me completely. I end much as I began, like the judge in one of F.E. Smith's cases, no wiser than before, but much better informed.

– Philip Pullman

Talking about Philosophy

Talking about Philosophy is a series of introductory philosophy books comprising interviews and essays from the world's leading philosophers. Here you can read the words of major thinkers such as Susan Blackmore, Patricia Churchland, Richard Dawkins, Frank Jackson, Steven Pinker and Peter Singer in connection to a single focused and knotty philosophical issue such as: how does the brain produce consciousness? How can we build a better society? Is it reasonable to believe in God?

Based on *The Panpsycast Philosophy Podcast*, each book takes the wisdom from the show's guests and puts their thoughts on the page, alongside and against one another. The series remasters the most pertinent and engaging selections from the conversations, presenting them alongside original essays from philosophy's biggest thinkers, and tying them together through the editor's expositions and critical commentaries. These are jargon-free guides to life's greatest questions.

Jack Symes

Jack Symes is a public philosopher and writer. He is the producer of *The Panpsycast Philosophy Podcast* and editor of the Bloomsbury series *Talking about Philosophy*. He is currently Teacher and Researcher at Durham University, UK.

Forthcoming titles include:

Philosophers on How to Live: Talking about Morality

www.thepanpsycast.com

Philosophers on God

Talking about Existence

Edited by Jack Symes

Assistant Editor: Casey Logue

BLOOMSBURY ACADEMIC
LONDON • NEW YORK • OXFORD • NEW DELHI • SYDNEY

BLOOMSBURY ACADEMIC
Bloomsbury Publishing Plc
50 Bedford Square, London, WC1B 3DP, UK
1385 Broadway, New York, NY 10018, USA
29 Earlsfort Terrace, Dublin 2, Ireland

BLOOMSBURY, BLOOMSBURY ACADEMIC and the Diana logo are trademarks
of Bloomsbury Publishing Plc

First published in Great Britain 2024

Series design by Louise Dugdale
Cover image © Syd Sujuaan/Unsplash

A catalogue record for this book is available from the British Library.

ISBN: HB: 978-1-3502-2729-3
PB: 978-1-3502-2730-9
ePDF: 978-1-3502-2731-6
eBook: 978-1-3502-2728-6

Series: Talking about Philosophy

Typeset by Deanta Global Publishing Services, Chennai, India
Printed and bound in Great Britain

To find out more about our authors and books visit www.bloomsbury.com and
sign up for our newsletters.

To my sisters and brother

Contents

Illustrations

All illustrations were created by Charlotte Mudd and are original to this work. Copyright of all illustrations is held by Jack Symes and Bloomsbury Publishing Plc.

Contributors

Susan Blackmore is Visiting Professor of Psychology at the University of Plymouth, UK.

William Lane Craig is Professor of Philosophy at Houston Christian University, USA.

Richard Dawkins is Emeritus Professor of the Public Understanding of Science at the University of Oxford, UK.

Daniel Dennett is Austin B. Fletcher Professor of Philosophy and Co-director of the Center for Cognitive Studies at Tufts University, USA.

Jessica Frazier is Lecturer in the Study of Religion at the University of Oxford, UK.

Daniel J. Hill is Senior Lecturer in Philosophy at the University of Liverpool, UK.

Silvia Jonas is Professor of Philosophy at the University of Bamberg, Germany.

Asha Lancaster-Thomas is Teacher of Philosophy at Atlanta Classical Academy, USA.

Stephen Law is Director of the Certificate in Higher Education and Director of Studies in Philosophy at the University of Oxford, Department of Continuing Education, UK.

Casey Logue is Teacher of English at Stamford School, UK.

Yujin Nagasawa is H. G. Wood Professor in Philosophy of Religion and Co-director of the Birmingham Centre for Philosophy of Religion at the University of Birmingham, UK.

Richard Swinburne is Emeritus Professor of Philosophy at the University of Oxford, UK.

Jack Symes is Teacher and Researcher of Philosophy at Durham University, UK.

Mohammad Saleh Zarepour is Lecturer in Philosophy at the University of Manchester, UK.

Acknowledgements

They say your second album is always the hardest. As it turns out, that's also true of books. When you're composing your first, there's a lifetime of learning, experiences and Adam Sandler jokes at your disposal; there's a profound sense of freedom that comes with the absence of rules and expectations. That all changes with the second. The success of the first book in this series, *Philosophers on Consciousness*, brought with it a whole host of new challenges. I worried that our fresh and exciting format would turn stale and what was once a comedic goldmine might become, as one reviewer put it, 'the unhinged persecution of one of America's greatest actors'. It turned out that, thanks to the book's contributors, I needn't have worried. I am delighted to present, *Philosophers on God: Talking about Existence*.

I would like to begin by thanking all of those who supported the production of *Philosophers on God*. Thank you to Thom Atkinson, Rose de Castellane, Andrew Horton, Oliver Marley and Gregory Miller for conducting the interviews within this series. Without their tireless enthusiasm, careful thinking and good humour, this book would not be possible. I am indebted to Charlotte Mudd for her illustrations and to Rose de Castellane for all of her encouragement and corrections. A special thank you to Casey Logue for preparing the original interview transcripts and, as ever, for her invaluable literary guidance.

I extend my deepest appreciation to the philosophers and scientists in this book, who have contributed tremendous time and thought to write essays, participate in interviews and edit their contributions at length. Working alongside people for whom I have such great admiration has been an enormous privilege; these are not just twelve of philosophy of religion's most influential thinkers, but some of the most dedicated and compassionate people I have come to know. On behalf of the contributors, thank you to Adam Bradbury, Martin Bradbury, Kristian Brindley, Rose de Castellane, Liam Cook, Harry Drummond, Philip Goff, Jonathon Hawkins, Simon Holland, Andrew Horton, Lucy James, Casey Logue, Oliver Marley, Gregory Miller, Mia Raszewski, Lauren Stephens, Maddison Symes, Samuel Symes, Stevie Symes, Paul Taylor and Emily Troscianko for their helpful comments on all or part of the text. I would also like to thank the anonymous reviewers at Bloomsbury for their thoughtful feedback throughout the book's various stages.

A tremendous thank you to those who have supported *The Panpsycast Philosophy Podcast* over the past eight years and, in particular, to our patrons whose charitable funding has allowed us to produce this book. I am also indebted to the Global Philosophy of Religion Project at the University of Birmingham – led by Yujin Nagasawa and generously funded by the John Templeton Foundation – for inspiring several of the book's themes and supporting the production of chapters three and four. On a personal note, I wish to express my gratitude to Durham University, the University of Chester and the University of Liverpool for supporting my research and writing. Much of this book was edited during my final months at the University of Liverpool, for which I owe the department and colleagues my heartfelt gratitude. I am indebted to my agent, Donald Winchester, as well as my mentors, Barry Dainton, Philip Goff, Daniel J. Hill and Emily Thomas, for their all-important guidance. Thank you to my family – Michelle, Gary, Alvin, Lisa, Stevie, Joshua, Ziggy, Freddie, Maddison, Adam, Autumn, Samuel, Mia, Rupert and Mollie – for imbuing my world with inspiration and love.

On behalf of all our contributors and readers, I reserve my earnest appreciation to Colleen Coalter, Suzie Nash, Becky Holland, Mohammed Raffi and Benedict O'Hagan at Bloomsbury. I thank them and the editorial board for the gift of this book's existence.

Preface

The clouds are grey, the sun obscured and you are walking through the countryside in the overcast of winter. Passing from field to woodland, the trees shed coats of frosty bark to celebrate the passing of another icy season. It feels too early for spring, but echoes of swallows in the canopies sing songs of new beginnings. You pause to catch a glimpse of your woodland companions. With effortless precision, your eyes track the birds as they zip between empty branches and, combining countless neurons, you forecast the birds' trajectory each time they fall out of view. Further down the bark-scattered path, a wooden bridge lies broken and burnt. As you near it, you see that its wounds were no mere accident: somebody wanted it to fall. You walk on, emerging from the trees, and return to the open fields. You look back, appreciate the woods and see a river flowing into the trees from the east. You squint, focusing your eyes on the horizon . . . Where does the river begin? Escaping the clouds, the sun will soon be free of the sky altogether; if you want to discover the river's source, you had better get walking.

The natural world is imbued with enormous complexity: trees respond to seasons, birds flap their wings, *Homo sapiens* build, burn and recognize moral facts and, when our minds reflect on such phenomena, we stand in admiration of their beauty. The wonders of the natural world are perplexing. Moreover, in order for the natural world to exist in the first place, there have to be complex *laws of* nature – a *precise* strength of gravity, a *constant* rate of cosmological expansion – from which the forest of life can emerge. Further still, there must be a *cause* to which these laws owe their existence: a source of the conditions for life, a well-spring of intricacy, a River of Eden and an origin of *existence*. That's the focus of this book: why there is something (a universe) rather than nothing, the reasons for the world's complexity, the purpose of our lives and the secrets of our futures.

Our guides to these questions are some of the world's most significant and influential thinkers. Each of the philosophers and scientists in this book has gone to extraordinary lengths to ensure that their work is communicated with elegance and ease. Whether you're an expert in philosophy or approaching this topic for the first time, I hope you find their ideas to be as clear as they are profound. Our twelve chapters are a mixture of essays and interviews. All of the essays are original to this book and represent some of the latest, most innovative research in the field. The interviews in this series were originally recorded for *The Panpsycast Philosophy Podcast*. Rest assured, you do not need to know anything about *The Panpsycast* to enjoy this book. Working alongside the contributors, these interviews have been completely remastered for the written page: the words have changed, the ideas updated and – where multiple interviewers conducted the original interviews – the format has been converted to one-on-one conversations.

From this point forward, when you see this heavier font being used in the body of the text, I am addressing you (the reader) or the interviewee. When the font is lighter, you're reading the words of the philosopher who is credited at the beginning of the relevant chapter. You'll also find some <u>info-boxes</u> throughout the book. Think of them like philosophical speed bumps; when the ideas are moving too fast, they slow down the discussion to ensure nobody's left behind. If you don't appreciate speed bumps, you can put your foot to the floor and fly right over them.

> The <u>info-boxes</u> look like this. Although, they're usually more informative!

As you explore the ideas within this book, I encourage you to challenge your own thoughts on the questions within it. The mysteries of existence are the greatest questions of all, and they impact every aspect of our being. In fact, whether or not you consider *God* to be a persuasive hypothesis might well be the most important decision you'll ever make.

Chapter One

Why God Matters

Daniel J. Hill

Introduction

Our journey begins with a straightforward question: why should we care about God? It doesn't seem to matter whether we believe in God or not, one might think, for it bears no impact on the things we find important. You're either religious or you're not and, if you're not, then that's fine; it's possible to live a meaningful, fulfilling and happy life without God. From this perspective, it can be difficult to see the value of deliberating the question of God's existence. If there's nothing at stake, then why waste our time? Perhaps this one is best left to the philosophers?

In our opening chapter, Daniel J. Hill guides us through the pitfalls of neglecting the God-question. As we shall see, Daniel is one of the most inspiring figures in philosophy of religion; his attention to detail is unrivalled and his passion for the topic is contagious. Hill is a committed Christian philosopher, whose work includes an extensive list of influential publications on the nature and existence of God. For Hill, there is no greater question than the nature of God's existence. The answer, he says, dictates life, death and everything in between.

To understand why God is important, we needn't appeal to abstract arguments concerning the nature of existence. All we need to do, thinks Hill, is reflect on the *possibility* that God might exist. If there's a chance that we're here for a reason, then there's hope for life after death – a life, one might think, of infinite happiness or eternal damnation. If God treats those who bury their heads in the sand no differently to those who purposefully reject Her, then you might as well place a bet – to reject God or not – and you better think carefully about it. We all have to wager. So, what's it going to be: believe or disbelieve? The dealer is waiting . . . 'Excuse me? It's time to place your bet.'

Life and death

Somebody once said to <u>Bill Shankly</u>, the iconic manager of Liverpool Football Club, 'Football is a matter of life and death to you.' Shankly replied, 'Listen, it's more important than that.'[1] Shankly may have been joking, but his words are literally true in connection to why God matters. This is because, if any of the <u>three major Western religions</u> is true, then whether we believe in God determines something much more important than life or death. Ultimately, it defines our final destination: whether we enjoy eternal happiness in heaven or suffer everlasting punishment in hell.

> <u>Bill Shankly</u> (1913–1981) is considered one of the greatest football managers in history. In 1959, Shankly took charge of the second division side 'Liverpool FC'. By 1981, at the end of Shankly's tenure, Liverpool had become one of Europe's most successful clubs.

> The <u>three major Western religions</u> are Judaism, Christianity and Islam. These faiths are also known as the 'Abrahamic religions', as they all believe in the same God: the God of the prophet Abraham.

Maybe you're not worried about heaven or hell; perhaps you don't think that any of the major world religions is true. Very well, but what are your *grounds* for thinking that? They had better be good grounds. After all, if we were playing Russian Roulette and I said – as I handed you the gun – 'I don't *think* that chamber six is loaded', then you'd want to know that I had very good reasons for my belief before you acted on it. Well, this is even more important, so you'd better make sure that your grounds are very, very good indeed.

You may be moved by this argument for the importance of wrestling with the question of God's existence, but you might be cynical about the prospects of success: 'If the greatest philosophers in history have not been able to agree on the question of God, then what hope do I have?' I think such pessimism is unjustified. We should keep in mind that even the greatest of thinkers can be wrong: Plato thought that most music and poetry should be banned,[2] Aristotle thought men had more teeth than women,[3] Bishop Berkeley thought everybody should drink <u>tar water</u>,[4, 5] Kant thought that cutting and selling hair was immoral,[6] Nietzsche thought it was wrong to drink alcohol,[7] and Wittgenstein thought that some detective thrillers contained more philosophy than professional journals.[8] (Mind you, there may be some truth to that last one.) I think that pretty much all of the great thinkers would agree that it's good to deliberate these questions for yourself. Most importantly, however, the Western religions say those who are neutral about God will be treated the same as those who reject Him. It's not enough to live a morally good life, say the traditional monotheisms, you have to believe in God as well. Therefore, dodging the question is a decidedly risky option.[9]

> In order to prevent diseases, such as smallpox and scurvy, George Berkeley (1685–1753) advised his readers to consume two glasses of <u>tar water</u> per day.
>
> A combination of tree resin and H_2O, tar water is renowned for its dark and sticky texture. In small, anti-scientific circles, tar water is considered healthy and delicious. Don't take our word for it; try some today!

The greatest possible being

Before we go any further, let's get clearer on what we mean by 'God'. When you think of 'God', the first image that comes to mind may be a wise-looking Santa Claus peeking through the clouds. Alternatively, you might think of God as the energy preceding the Big Bang, Morgan Freeman in *Bruce Almighty* or a toga-wearing giant at the gates of heaven. One famous definition among philosophers of religion is that 'God' means 'the greatest possible being': a being that isn't just greater than every other being that *actually* exists, but greater than every other being that *could* have existed. This definition has a lot of force to it. Suppose someone said to you, 'I believe in God but, to be honest, I don't think God's actually that great. There are, or could have been, many greater things than God.' You might think that your friend didn't know what the word 'God' meant . . . maybe they were confused, or English wasn't their first language. You'd respond in the same way if your friend told you they'd seen a triangle with four sides: you'd think they were messing with you, or that they didn't know what the word 'triangle' meant. You would react in this way because, just as we all have a shared understanding of what a triangle is, we all have a shared idea of God. There might be a lot of disagreements about God, and there may even be disagreements about triangles, but there are some things we can agree on. Pretty much everyone agrees that *if* God exists, then He must be greater than any other being that has existed, does exist or could have existed.

'It's all very well saying that God is "the greatest possible being", but that doesn't tell us very much. What is it, exactly, that makes a being *great*?' This is an important question, and philosophers disagree on the answer, but I think there are some attributes on which most of us can agree. Suppose you're walking down a street and come across a burning house – the roof is collapsing and, inside, dogs are barking and people are screaming. You're the only person around who can help. So, what are you going to rescue first? The people? The dogs? The ornaments? Before anything else, I'd save the human occupants, and I reckon you'd do the same. I'd do it because I think that human beings are more important than pets or artefacts. It's not because the people would be grateful to me; if I'd never met them, and knew I'd never meet them again, I'd still choose to save them. There's something in the nature of human beings, it seems to me, which makes them more worthy of saving than pets or artefacts. Of course, after I saved the humans, I'd go back for the pets, but the ornaments would be last on my list. Why? Because dogs and human beings – who have even richer mental lives – are conscious and, to put it simply, it's *greater* to be conscious than not.

> We all know what consciousness is: it's the *fear* of death, the *taste* of tar water and the *confusion* of falling ill. If something is <u>conscious</u>, then there's *something that it's like* to *be* that being.

Another way of looking at this is to consider a game invented by the philosopher <u>Nelson Pike</u>.[10] Pike asks us to imagine two doors, behind each of which is an object. Our job is to save one object and destroy the other. Here's the catch: the only information we have about each object is what's written on the doors. Now, suppose that on one door it says 'conscious' and on the other door it says 'not conscious'. Which object would you save, and which would you destroy?

> <u>Nelson Pike</u> (1930–2010) was an enormously influential philosopher of religion. His most famous book, *God and Timelessness* (1970) is considered essential reading for anybody who is interested in the nature and attributes of God.

It seems to me that the right thing to do, given the limited information we have, is to preserve the object that is conscious. You may object: 'To be honest, there are some conscious beings that I'd rather not save. For example, I *hate* flies. They're *very* annoying!' That's a fair point. Flies are annoying, and consciousness isn't the only thing that's relevant when we're deciding whether or not to save something. For example, if something has the potential to harm by carrying disease, or even just the potential to annoy, then that may be a reason to destroy it. It's also worth noting that some conscious things (such as dogs) seem to have a richer mental life than others (like flies). So, if one door reads 'rich mental life' and the other 'non-rich mental life', then I'd save the being with the rich mental life. (That is, on the assumption that the other being didn't have the *potential* for a rich mental life.) You may, quite understandably, object to this as well. 'There are some things with rich mental lives that I'd prefer *not* to save; Joseph Stalin and Adam Sandler, for example.' To say this, I believe, is to acknowledge that – as well as there being some features that enhance greatness – there are some features that detract from greatness. In the case of Stalin and Sandler, this would be moral wickedness and displeasing artistry. On the positive side, moral goodness (or pleasing artistry) enhances greatness. Let's put this in terms of Pike's game. Suppose that the only information on the doors were this: the object behind door number one is 'morally good' and the object behind door number two is 'not morally good'. Which would you save? The right thing to do, it seems, would be to preserve the entity behind door number one – to save the morally good thing over that which is not morally good.

Now we have a couple of suggestions for what God will be like. First, God has the property that puts human beings and pets above artefacts: consciousness. Second, God has the property that puts saints above Stalin: the property of moral goodness. We can extend this process further to fill out the concept of God. For example, playing Pike's game, we can say that God will also be all-powerful, all-knowing and perfectly free. Of course, none of this is to assume that there's *actually* a God; we're just talking about the *idea* of God. It is similar to what you'd say to a friend who asked you, 'How many horns does a unicorn have?' You'd reply, 'One.' This wouldn't mean that you believed in unicorns; it just means that you understand the *idea* of a unicorn . . . and that you and your friend are struggling for interesting topics of conversation.

Gambling on God

'Now I have an idea of God, but I still don't see why God matters. To be honest, I don't really care whether He exists or not; I'm an <u>apatheist</u>!' Is this a reasonable position to hold? Not according to the seventeenth-century mathematician <u>Blaise Pascal</u>.[11] Pascal recognized that it's hard to be certain whether God exists; he insisted that this shouldn't lead to practical inactivity, however. According to Pascal, everyone faces the same choice: to gamble on God or not.

What do you stand to gain or lose? Let's say there's a fifty-fifty chance that God exists – it's just as likely that God exists than not. Suppose you believe in God and live your earthly life according to God's principles, and it turns out that God *actually* exists. Well, what will you gain? According to Judaism, Christianity and Islam, you'll be rewarded with heaven: everlasting happiness. Now, what will happen if you believe in God and live your earthly life according to God's principles, but it turns out that God *doesn't* actually exist? I don't think you'll lose out on much. Maybe you'll miss out on having everything *your* way in this life – trading church for a few more hours in bed – but that doesn't bear comparison with what you might gain. After all, this

> A 'theist' believes that God exists, an 'atheist' claims that God does *not* exist, an 'agnostic' doesn't commit to either position and an apatheist just doesn't care – they're apathetic!

> Blaise Pascal (1623–1662) was a prolific mathematician, philosopher and physicist. Today, he is best-known for his contributions to probability theory, 'Pascal's triangle' and – the argument that Hill puts forward in this chapter – 'Pascal's wager'.

life lasts for only a few decades, while everlasting happiness lasts, well, for ever! That's the thing about heaven's being everlasting: even the slightest chance of *eternal* happiness should be preferred over any amount of *finite* happiness.

Let's consider the other side of the coin. What do you stand to *lose* if God exists, and you don't care or don't believe? (For Pascal, being apathetic about God is the same as not believing.) Well, according to the Western monotheisms, you run the risk of everlasting punishment in hell.[12] You may not believe in hell, but the point isn't whether you believe in hell or not. The point is whether you think that there's *a risk* of hell. Suppose that you accept there is *some* risk – let's say there's a one per cent chance. Weighed up against the risk of everlasting punishment, what is the potential gain? A few decades of pleasure? It might be worth risking a lifetime of partying and disbelief for a one per cent chance of 5,000 years of punishment, but it definitely isn't worth risking (even at a one per cent chance) *everlasting* punishment in hell. That's the way with eternity: no finite pleasure is worth even the risk of infinite suffering.

The conclusion of 'Pascal's wager' is this: whether God exists or not, it doesn't make sense for us not to believe. To return to our earlier example, betting against the existence of God would be like betting that the gun with three loaded chambers won't kill you. You have very little to gain, but – as one might put it – a *hell* of a lot to lose.

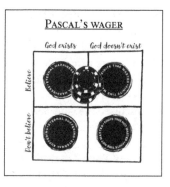

The meaningful life

If life just evolved out of non-living matter without any purpose or guidance, there is a sense in which life is meaningless. On atheism, life has no more meaning than a random arrangement of leaves being blown about by the wind. Such an arrangement might *look* meaningful – let's say, if the leaves seemed to spell out a word – but it wouldn't *be* meaningful unless God or someone were manipulating the leaves. 'Sure', you might say, 'life as a *whole* isn't meaningful, but *my* life is meaningful. My family, friends and FarmVille: these are all things that *I* find meaningful!'[13] That might be right, but if God does exist, not only is your life meaningful, but its meaning fits in with the reason for your creation. What's more, if you have doubts about whether you have chosen the correct or best meaning for your own life – you don't know the future, after all, and you

> FarmVille© is a free-to-play agricultural simulator. Released in 2009, FarmVille is celebrated for its biodiversity and compelling social gameplay.

might not be the best judge of your own gifts and talents – then the existence of God would guarantee an unshakeable meaning that would constitute the best meaning that life could have. The same applies to fulfilment. Fulfilment is not the same as *happiness* but refers to a more deep-seated longer-term sense of satisfaction with one's role in the world. Theists say that belief makes their lives more fulfilling: if you believe that God loves you and has a plan for your life, then that makes your role in the world more secure. There is more to life than happiness. Even if the lives of doctors, soldiers, firefighters, aid workers, freedom fighters and care workers were unhappy, we'd still consider their lives to be profoundly important – if not more valuable than the lives of those who choose to focus on their own contentment. Living a genuinely fulfilled and meaningful life is probably more important than being happy . . . though, of course, I hope you'll be happy as well.

Perhaps none of this moves you; maybe you're one hundred per cent sure that there isn't a God, so there's nothing to gamble or benefit from. Still, I think it would be unreasonable to say that the question didn't matter. Even if you're determined to stick to your guns, it's still going to be worth investigating the *greatest* idea that humans have ever created – or, as I think, was revealed to them. Pretty much every one of humanity's great thinkers has discussed the God-question in one way or another. Isaac Newton wrote more on religious matters than he did on science and Johann Sebastian Bach had a personal library of fifty-two books on theology.[14, 15] Understanding the world we inhabit is valuable in its own right. The God-question goes further, however: it doesn't just ask us what *does* exist, but what *could* exist or what could *never* exist. Questions of God are intimately connected with questions of meaning, morality, mathematics, consciousness and the origin of the cosmos. This topic may offer rewards that are, quite literally, out of this world. Yet, I promise – like the great minds that came before – you will find enormous value in the journey itself, in the here and now, at every twist and turn.

> It's not unusual for Johann Sebastian Bach (1685–1750) to be described as 'the greatest composer of all time'. Compared to his contemporaries, Bach's theological library was extensive, and much bigger than his collection on music.

Afterthoughts

To dismiss God's existence from the outset is more than a little foolish; it's entirely reckless. If you're going to gamble on an *eternity* of suffering without a moment's reflection, then I'll not be trusting you to prescribe my medicine or fix my car. Pascal's wager may not convince us to believe in God, but it shows that it's all worth thinking about. If there is *any* chance that one of the Abrahamic religions is true, then there's a chance of hell. We need to ask ourselves if it's a risk we ought to take.

It's unclear, however, whether religion is the sort of thing we can just gamble on. Having faith, you might think, is something that develops naturally. You can't just 'choose to believe' like you would 'choose to bet' and, even if you could, I doubt that God would appreciate being treated like a racehorse. You can't just *say* you believe in God; somehow, you'd have to form a genuine belief. Take this book as a stepping stone: if there is even the faintest chance that reading this will lead you towards belief in God, resulting in your everlasting happiness, then maybe it will be worth it.

All of this is to assume that the Abrahamic religions have some degree of credibility. Of course, it may turn out that none of them – or a non-Western religion – may be true. In either case, before we place our bets, we ought to assign probabilities. Pascal tells us to wager 'without hesitating' . . . he may have had a gambling problem.[16,17] Eternal existence could be impossible, unlimited power may be incoherent and an all-loving god might be unable to create a place of infinite suffering. Let's gamble responsibly; let's take a breath and calculate the odds before we wager.

Questions to consider

1. How important is the question of God's existence?
2. What properties would the 'greatest possible being' possess?
3. Does Pascal's wager demonstrate that Western monotheism is the only rational choice?
4. How much probability would you assign to God's existence?
5. Is life more meaningful under theism than atheism?

Recommended reading

Advanced

Daniel Hill, *Divinity and Maximal Greatness* (London: Routledge, 2005).

> This is Hill's defence of perfect-being theology. Here, he explores the nature of 'maximal greatness' and argues that the attributes associated with this idea – such as omnipotence, omniscience and omnibenevolence – sufficiently capture God's divinity. This book is aimed at professional philosophers and high-ability graduate students.

Blaise Pascal, *Pensées and Other Writings*, trans. Honor Levi, ed. Anthony Levi (Oxford: Oxford University Press, 2008).

> If you want to grapple with Pascal's argument first-hand, then this is definitely worth reading – the wager is only a couple of pages long. The *Pensées* ('thoughts'), a name given to the text after Pascal's death, was intended to be his greatest work; however, the book was never completed. Instead, what we have is a series of fragments defending the Christian faith.

<u>Intermediate</u>

Brian Davies, *An Introduction to the Philosophy of Religion*, 4th edition (Oxford: Oxford University Press, 2020).

> The first edition of Davies's book was published in 1997. Since then, it has become *the* core text for students of philosophy of religion. If you're studying for an exam – or you're looking for a concise and informative guide to Western philosophy of religion – then it's worth picking up a copy. Davies also has another excellent study guide, *Philosophy of Religion: A Guide and Anthology*,[18] a collection of sixty-five short essays and extracts from some of philosophy's most influential historical (and some contemporary) thinkers.

T. J. Mawson, *Belief in God: An Introduction to the Philosophy of Religion* (Oxford: Oxford University Press, 2005).

> Mawson's introduction offers a delightful overview of the nature of God and all of the central arguments for (and against) God's existence. Perfect for the general reader, Mawson's personal, profound and (often) witty writing style sets this book apart.

<u>Beginner</u>

Tim Bayne, *Philosophy of Religion: A Very Short Introduction* (Oxford: Oxford University Press, 2018).

> Bayne's book is a great place to start; it's a brief and general introduction to the field, covering a surprising number of perspectives and questions. The chapters on divine hiddenness and the afterlife are uniquely brilliant.

Justin Brierley, *Unbelievable?: Why after ten years of talking with atheists, I'm still a Christian* (London: SPCK, 2017).

> Brierley hosted Premier Christian Radio's flagship programme – *Unbelievable?* – for over a decade. This book is not just an insightful personal reflection: it's an engaging, first-rate defence of the Christian faith.

Chapter Two

The Coherence of Theism

Richard Swinburne

Introduction

Take a moment to reflect on some of humanity's greatest discoveries: the Big Bang, vaccinations, electricity, evolution by natural selection. It's undeniable that science – by explaining physical objects and their powers – has made incredible progress. Understandably, this has given the public great trust in the scientific method and its ability to deliver a comprehensive theory of reality. However, if we treat the universe as an entirely physical phenomenon, and reject the possibility of supernatural causes, then perhaps our understanding of reality will always be limited. If the simplest explanation of the world is offered by something other than physical science, then we'll need to broaden our minds.

Our first interviewee, Richard Swinburne, thinks we need to do just that: look beyond physical science. Swinburne's acclaimed trilogy – *The Coherence of Theism*,[1] *The Existence of God*,[2] and *Faith and Reason*[3] – are three of the most influential texts in the history of philosophy of religion and, consequently, his work is essential reading for anybody working in the field. For Swinburne, religious belief is the friend, not the enemy, of modern thinking. From the mystery of the universe's existence and the finely tuned laws which operate within it, to its conscious creatures and extraordinary miracles: it is theism, says Swinburne, which offers the best explanation of the world.

In this chapter, we'll be exploring the concept and explanatory power of God. There are many who claim that the concept of God is logically incoherent. It is not possible, they argue, for a being to be all-powerful, all-knowing and all-loving; for them, believing in God is like believing in 'square-circles' or 'funny Adam Sandler movies'. Swinburne, who defends the coherence of God's attributes against several popular objections, addresses this concern and proceeds to develop a cumulative <u>inductive</u> argument for the existence of God. Each argument, says Swinburne, increases the probability of

> A (successful) <u>inductive</u> argument shows that its conclusion is *highly likely* – but not guaranteed – to be true. In contrast, a (successful) deductive argument proves that its conclusion is – not just probably true, but – *definitely* true.

God and – taken together – makes God's existence more probable than not.

The big picture

Before we explore the concept and existence of God, I wonder what you think about the purpose of philosophy more generally. How would you describe 'philosophy' and its relationship with science?

I see philosophy as the study of the deepest questions and their deepest explanations; it explores mysteries like why there is a universe, why there are certain laws of nature, why the world contains conscious beings, whether there are moral truths and how we can know what they are. Stated more formally, philosophy aims to discover the <u>necessary</u> truths of *any* universe and the <u>contingent</u> truths of *this* universe. Science, on the other hand, sets itself up to explain a specific type of phenomenon: our physical universe at a particular point in time. It provides these explanations in terms of how the universe existed at an earlier time and how the laws of nature operate, but it is not a complete explanation. If you want a complete explanation of the world, then science won't give you one; to grasp the bigger picture, we need to explain why there is a universe at all, why there are laws of nature in the first place and why there are *these* laws of nature rather than other ones. That's where philosophy comes in.

> A <u>necessary</u> truth is something that could *not* have been otherwise. For example, no matter how the universe was formed, two plus two would always equal four.

> A <u>contingent</u> truth is something that *could* have been otherwise. For example, it's true that Joni Mitchell wrote the hit song *Big Yellow Taxi*, but she didn't *have* to write it. After all, there might have been no *Big Yellow Taxi* or (God forbid) no Joni Mitchell.

How and why did you become interested in these deeper questions?

From my teenage years, I have always been interested in answering philosophical questions for their own sake. It's important to know whether my answers to these questions are true; and, if they are true, whether I can give other people reasons for believing them. With that said, I also think we should explore these questions because they're crucial to showing us how we ought to live in the world. For example, if you think that God exists, then this raises the importance of living a good life in the here and now. In terms of religious questions, for as long as I can remember, I've always believed that God exists. In my mid-twenties, I was inspired by the medieval scholastic tradition of giving reasoned arguments for God and the doctrines of the Christian religion, and I was pleased to find that in this endeavour I shared some of Aquinas's ambitions. In those earlier years, the *Summa Theologiae* was a big inspiration!

> Saint Thomas Aquinas (1225–1274) is one of Christianity's most notable philosophers. He is best-known for his unfinished masterpiece, the *Summa Theologiae* (1265–), in which he sought to reconcile his religious beliefs with the (Aristotelian) philosophy of his time.

If your belief in God has remained solid, I wonder, have there been any big shifts in other areas of your thinking?

I think about this quite a bit. I admire people who have a belief, who are open to counterarguments and change their views in the light of the evidence. We should encourage this kind of intellectual honesty and praise those who are influenced by truth and reason. I have deepened my views on many things. For example, when I first started thinking about these issues, I had no idea about the nature of scientific explanations, about the criteria for a probably true explanation and how these support the case for God. In truth, there haven't been any 'big' shifts in the overall framework of my beliefs. Each time I go through my arguments for God's existence, I ask myself whether they're sound or whether I just don't like changing my mind. All I can say is, I hold these views because I think they're true!

Stones, sins and cereals

I'd like to begin with the concept of 'God'. When you use the word 'God', what sort of being are you referring to?

When I'm talking about 'God', I'm referring to what the Christian tradition has always meant. For Christians, God is the perfectly free, personal being who created the universe; He is omnipotent in that He can do everything that's logically possible to do, omniscient in the sense that He knows everything that is logically possible to know and is perfectly good in that He always does the best action when there is a best action to do – otherwise, God will perform a good action, but never a bad action. That's what I mean by 'God'.

Many atheists claim that this conception of God is incoherent. For example, some question whether it's possible for any being to be 'omnipotent'. This, they say, is illustrated through the paradox of the stone, which asks whether God could create a stone so heavy that no being could lift it. If the answer is 'yes, God could create the stone', then there is something which God cannot do (that is, lift the stone); however, if the answer is no, then there is something *else* that God cannot do (namely, create the stone). How would you respond to this paradox?

This needs to be spelled out rather carefully. The normal Christian view is that God has, with one exception, all the properties which I have just listed *essentially* – that is to say, God couldn't exist without these properties. It's an essential property of my desk that it occupies space; if it ceased to occupy space, then it would cease to exist. Similarly, an essential property of a triangle is that it has three sides; if it didn't have three sides, then it wouldn't be a triangle. Apart from being creator of the universe, which is a contingent property of God, all of those properties of God which I have listed are essential in this same way.

Now, in response to the paradox of the stone, my answer is as follows: no, God cannot create a stone that is too heavy for him to lift. It is logically impossible to do so because that would bring about God existing without omnipotence, which is one of His essential properties. It's important to keep in mind the definition of 'omnipotence' that I gave a moment ago – that to be omnipotent is to have the power to bring about any logically possible state of affairs. Not being able to do the logically impossible isn't a limitation on God, because a logically impossible action is not an action that it makes sense to suppose that *any* agent could perform. Therefore, just as my inability to draw a square-circle isn't a lack of power on my part, God lacks nothing in not being able to create an unliftable stone.

Cynics also maintain that God's properties are in tension with one another. For example, some argue that because God is perfectly good, God does not have 'the *power* to sin' and, therefore, can't be all-powerful. What do you make of this argument? Do you think that God has the power to sin?

If by 'sin' you mean 'do what is morally wrong', then no, God cannot sin. Nevertheless, I don't think this is a problem for God. As I've said, one of God's essential properties is that He's perfectly good and always chooses the best action. If there isn't a possible best action, then God might do an action which is not the best, but He couldn't sin. Again, this is because perfect goodness is an essential property of God and, therefore, it is not logically possible for God to do a morally wrong action.

If you're right – and we accept that God's nature is internally coherent – I wonder if God's properties might contradict facts about the world. To take one example, Christians usually believe that humans possess free will, which consists in having the power to determine our futures. However, if God knows everything, then God knows what I'm going to do in the future, so I don't have the power to alter my path. Does this force Christians to choose between human free will and God's omniscience?

I don't think so, but this is a much-contested issue. Let's suppose that God had a view today about what I will do tomorrow: suppose He knew that I was going to have Corn Flakes for my breakfast. If God believed I was going to pour myself a bowl of Corn Flakes, but in a moment of spontaneity I chose the Crunchy Nut instead, this would make God's previous belief false.[4] However, because God is omniscient, He can't have any false beliefs. Recall that when I described God as 'omniscient', I said that this means He

> Crunchy Nut© is a flake-based breakfast cereal; their honey drizzle and peanut topping make them, well, irresistibly tasty.

knows everything that is logically possible to know. Now, in short, that's my response: I don't think that it's logically possible for anybody to know what a future free agent will do and that's why God cannot know our futures. This does not mean that God lacks anything. There are only free agents because God gives some agents the gift of free will.

I should point out that my view presupposes that God exists in time, that there's a history to God, and this is a hotly contested issue. Some people are determined to show that God exists outside of time. Personally, I don't see how this conception of God – who knows timelessly what every agent is ever going to do – can be reconciled with the existence of free will. With that said, even if one *could* explain how free agents are compatible with a timeless God, then this would still be an unattractive picture of him. Those who think that God is outside of time overlook the fact that theists believe they can interact with God. When I do something bad, God is angry with me; when I say sorry, God forgives me. These are successive events – one is in response to the other – however, if it's all 'foreknown' by a God who exists outside of time, then I can't be interacting with him. In my view, that's not the best kind of God there could be.

The simplest solution

According to many atheists, the universe is a <u>brute fact</u>. There is no God, and we're extremely lucky that the laws of nature provide the conditions required for the development of intelligent life. Why is it, Richard, that you think your explanation of the universe is more appealing?

Better put, I think that it's not merely 'more appealing', but more probably true. It is important to understand how we select between competing theories. You only ever have a finite amount of evidence in favour of any scientific or historical theory (for example, there is only a finite amount of evidence for gravity, or for believing that Egyptians built the pyramids) and there will always be an infinite number of theories which

> A <u>brute fact</u> is the most fundamental type of explanation that one can give. This is the point at which no deeper explanation can be provided – that is to say, when something can't be explained in terms of something else.

can accommodate such evidence (fairies could force objects to the ground, and aliens could have placed the pyramids in Egypt). While some further piece of evidence may eliminate many such theories, there will still be an infinite number of theories remaining. In science and history, therefore, we're not just looking for theories that fit the evidence. The further criterion, which scientists and historians use in determining which theory is most probable, is the criterion of simplicity. I have analysed at length what makes one theory simpler than another theory. My conclusion is that one is simpler than another insofar as it postulates fewer entities, fewer easily observable or experienceable properties, and mathematically simple relations between these.

To understand why postulating God as a brute fact is simpler than postulating the universe and its physical laws as brute facts, let's consider what we mean by a 'law of nature'. A law of nature is a true statement about the powers and <u>liabilities</u> of entities. So, when we say, 'the law of gravity operates throughout the universe', we mean that every fundamental particle has the property of attracting every other fundamental particle. To explain this phenomenon, <u>naturalists</u> – that is, atheists – postulate as brute facts an enormous number of fundamental particles which have exactly the same properties. (Alternatively, they may postulate an <u>initial singularity</u> or primaeval soup made of an enormous number of parts, each of which has the same power to produce fundamental particles with the same powers.) That's not a simple starting point. In fact, it's far from it: it's an enormously complex coincidence of an enormous number of entities with exactly the same powers!

> Simply put, <u>liabilities</u> are the forces that entities are subject to. Here, Swinburne's argument is that atheism must assume that *every single particle in the universe* 'just so happens' to have the same powers and liabilities. On theism, however, there is a simpler explanation for this apparent coincidence: God.

> It is typical for <u>naturalists</u> to believe that everything in existence is physical. Naturalists don't believe in supernatural entities like gods and ghosts.

> The <u>initial singularity</u> is the entity that existed before the Big Bang; this singularity is said to have contained all of space and time.

Let's contrast this story with that of theists. According to theism, every object that exists – apart from God Himself – is caused to exist and is held in existence by God. This means that every property or power that a substance possesses is caused or allowed to occur by God. Therefore, unlike the atheist – whose ultimate explanation attributes the existence of the universe and its operation in accordance with simple laws to an enormous number of entities that, coincidentally, just so happen to have the same properties – the theist can explain the existence and orderliness of the universe by a much simpler hypothesis: God.

As a person rather than a physical mechanism, did God *choose* to create the world in this way? If so, then what was God's motivation?

Yes, God did choose to create the world, and I think the theist can explain why God would bring about a universe with simple laws of a kind that lead to the existence of conscious human beings. God is perfectly good and omnipotent and, therefore, He is likely to create humans because they are good things. Humans have a kind of goodness which even God Himself does not have: the goodness of being able to choose between good and evil. If there are to be humans, in order for them to have bodies through which they can interact with each other, there needs to be a physical universe: simple laws which give rise to simple regularities, the evolution of human bodies, human consciousness and laws which people can understand and manipulate. The atheist cannot explain why the universe exists in this way.

In their defence, the atheist just believes in physical processes, but theists assume the existence of all these additional, non-physical entities: God, souls, angels and the like. How would you respond to the claim that your explanation relies too heavily on strange and peculiar entities?

Science is always postulating strange entities, hitherto unknown and not available in observable sizes, in order to explain the behaviour of objects that are observable. It introduced atoms, which nobody could see at the time, to explain why certain substances combine in certain ratios by weight and volume to make other substances. At first, this seemed like a nice, simple picture; but then new phenomena turned up and science had to introduce yet more fundamental particles, such as protons, neutrons, photons and the like. It began to be the case that, at the quantum level, these things have some very strange properties. These fundamental particles are both, in a sense, particles and, in another sense, waves. But so long as you get the right results, and the theory is fairly simple, then we have reason for believing that these theories are true, and the same applies to the existence of God.

You describe God as a 'simple hypothesis', but isn't God quite a significant and complex assumption?

I used to say that believing in God is simple because it involves hypothesizing one person who possesses three properties: essential everlasting omnipotence, omniscience and perfect freedom.[5] From these three properties, I used to say that we can deduce all of God's other attributes. These days, however, I think that God is even simpler because we can deduce God's nature from just one central property: essential everlasting omnipotence.

God is omnipotent, which means He has unlimited power. There are zero limits to this power – and zero is a very simple number. God is everlasting, meaning there are zero limits to the length of His life. God wouldn't be truly omnipotent unless He's perfectly free to do anything that's logically possible and, therefore, God must be perfectly free. A perfectly free being will not be subject to irrational desires; hence, if God sees that some action is the best available to Him – or one of the equal best available to Him – inevitably He'll perform it. Otherwise, if there is no best or equal best action, then God will do some good action, because to recognize an action as 'good' means that you have some inclination to do it. Of course, we humans are subject to irrational desires; we have desires which incline us to do what we recognize as bad and, therefore, we don't always do what's best. However, God is not subject to irrational desires and will always do as good an action as possible, and so God will be perfectly good. Furthermore, a being will only be truly omnipotent if He knows the consequences of His actions. Finally, everything that's happened in the past entails that every future action will have a certain property. Consider an example: 'John having been born in 1990' entails that if John lives for forty years, he will be forty years old in 2030. Therefore, God will know that among His choices in 2025 include the choice of allowing John to live until he's forty years old or causing him to die before he reaches the age of forty. God will also know that in 2025 He does not have the choice of causing John to die before he reaches the age of thirty, because in 2025, John would be thirty-five. What applies to that example applies generally: God will only know the choices available to Him in the future if He knows everything that has happened in the past. Likewise, in order to know what choices are open to Him, God must know which actions are logically impossible; therefore, He must know all of the logically necessary truths. All of this follows from the idea that there is an omnipotent being, and that is a very simple hypothesis.

You haven't mentioned God's necessity: the belief that God exists in every possible world. Do you think that God *does* exist in every possible world?

I don't think that God exists in every possible world. However, it's important to understand what that means. When I say, 'God does not exist in every possible world', I'm not suggesting that there's an *actual* world in which God doesn't exist. Possible worlds are a philosopher's invention. When philosophers say something does or does not exist in a possible world, they just mean that that thing is or is not logically possible. I think that a world without God is logically possible – it doesn't contain any contradictions – but I don't think that

When philosophers discuss possible worlds, they're just talking about how the world could (or could not) have been. For example, the world could have contained more mango trees (so there *is* a possible world with more mango trees), but it couldn't have contained square-circles (so there *isn't* a possible world with square-circles).

has any profound implications. All that means is that there exists a sentence, 'there is no God', which doesn't entail a contradiction. This shouldn't worry believers because in this world – that is, the world that we actually occupy – God offers the best explanation for the existence and order of the cosmos.

It is sometimes suggested that a scientific hypothesis is only rendered probable by evidence if, after it has been formulated, it successfully predicts new observations. The benefit of physical science is that it provides testable hypotheses, and testability appears to be an important theoretical virtue. The God-hypothesis doesn't seem to offer us any testable predictions. Is this a limitation of theism?

That seems false to me. A consequence of your suggestion would be that if a scientist has, for example, twenty pieces of observed evidence which are explained by a simple hypothesis, when that same hypothesis predicts a twenty-first observation, then the hypothesis becomes *more probable* than it would have been if the scientist had already observed the twenty-first piece of evidence. That seems wrong. *When* a scientific theory is formulated, or the *motive* of the scientist for making the observation, can hardly make a difference to the probability of a hypothesis on a certain body of evidence. The only thing that can matter is whether the evidence the scientist has makes the hypothesis probable. Of course, scientists understandably look for more evidence, and the more evidence a theory will explain, the greater the probability of its truth; however, scientists may already have enough evidence to label a hypothesis as true, and I claim that this is the case with the hypothesis that there is a God.

More generally, it is often suggested that a 'scientific' hypothesis must be 'testable' – that it must be possible to check whether a theory is true. Given that we can't test for the existence of supernatural entities, such as souls and angels, does this make believing in God anti-scientific?

I see no justification for that claim. For example, there seems to be no way of testing scientific hypotheses about how galaxies behave beyond the <u>event horizon</u>, although that hypothesis may constitute the simplest conclusion from evident data about how galaxies behave in the region which we can observe. Note too that there is often no way of testing some hypothesis in historical or forensic

> The <u>event horizon</u> is a region in space too far away from us for light, or any other signal from it, to ever reach us.

inquiry, yet these disciplines are not considered 'unscientific' for this reason.

Thus, there is often no way of testing an otherwise very probable hypothesis about who killed some ancient pharaoh: although, of course, some relevant new piece of evidence may (or may not) turn up unexpectedly. I see no reason for claiming that in this respect the hypothesis that there is a God is unscientific.

God revealed

Let's move on to another specific type of evidence: religious experience. You have argued elsewhere that religious experiences – such as hearing the voice of God – provide strong evidence for God's existence.[6] How do you justify such a claim?

To be more precise, what I have claimed is that seeming to hear the voice of God provides *some* evidence for God's existence. If the experiences are very powerful such that it seems overwhelmingly evident that these experiences are of God, then they would provide – for those who had the experience – strong evidence for His existence. Those of us who have only fairly weak experiences of God would only be justified in believing that those experiences coincide with reality if we had no reason to suppose that there is no God. However, the more positive evidence of other kinds we have for the existence of God, the more probable it is that the apparent experience of Him is a genuine one; therefore, I say, these experiences provide *additional* evidence for God's existence.

Why do you think we should prefer supernatural explanations of religious experiences over naturalistic ones, such as drugs or drunkenness?

What I have just asserted follows from what I call the 'principle of credulity', which states that a person is always justified in believing that things are how they seem to be – that is, in the absence of contrary evidence. If we didn't accept this principle, we wouldn't be justified in believing in anything, since ultimately all of our beliefs are based on the way things seem to be to us. For example, if it seems to me that there's a tree in front of me, I ought to believe there's a tree in front of me – in the absence of evidence that I am subject to a delusion. The same applies if I believe that God is talking to me; however, if I have some reason to believe that there isn't a God, then I would require further positive evidence for the existence of God in order to believe that the experience is genuine. If a religious experience is just an experience of the presence of God and no more than that, then given that there is a God, the experience is ultimately caused by God as He is the ultimate cause of whatever in the brain is causing us to have this experience. Necessarily, then, given that there is a God, this will be a veridical experience. On the other hand, if the experience contains ungodly material, such as God apparently commanding me to kill innocent people, then I would not be justified in attributing the experience to God. I know that a perfectly good being is not going to issue that sort of commandment.

There are some things that we believe on the basis of people's testimonies. However, if somebody told us that God was talking to them, would it not be reasonable to suspect a lie?

Following what I call the 'principle of testimony', we should believe what other people tell us – again, in the absence of evidence that what they say is false or that they could not know what they're telling us. Therefore, we should believe that those who claim they have experienced God have indeed had these experiences, unless we have reason to doubt their claims. Again, the principle of testimony is a principle we use in life more generally, and I see no reason why it shouldn't apply here too. All else being equal – for example, in the absence of reason to believe that our informants are liars – we should believe that people probably did experience what they tell us. This is true, even if we do have *some* reason for doubting the existence of God; since a great many people have had religious experiences, these experiences increase the probability that God exists. After all, it is to be expected that if God exists, He will choose to manifest His presence to some of the humans that He has created.

The good place

If God is perfectly good, then it seems that God would create a *good* world rather than an *evil* world and, in your written work, you have claimed this is exactly the kind of universe that we find ourselves in. 'Life is a tremendous good in itself', you say, and within life 'the good things outweigh the bad'.[7] How can you justify such a belief, given that the world contains so much pain and suffering?

There are a few things to say here. First, we should recognize that – on the whole – people want to exist. I think this says a lot about our assessment of the world. Even most people who are suffering want to go on living, even when life is painful. On the whole, they take the good to outweigh the bad.

The problem of evil, however, is why an all-loving, all-powerful and perfectly good God would allow us to suffer at all. In answering this question, we should begin by distinguishing 'natural' evils from 'moral' evils. Natural evils are those evils that are outside of our control. In contrast, moral evils are those which are caused by human beings deliberately or through negligence. God could have created a universe in which human beings could only do good and could never do evil, but then we wouldn't have any responsibility for things going well. In giving us free will, God trusts us (within limits) with His universe and wants us to care for the world and each other. It's a great gift that we're responsible for other people; serious responsibility involves making an effort to benefit others rather than harm them or let them suffer through our negligence. Our having this great responsibility necessarily involves the possibility of others suffering. Furthermore, through our choosing between good or evil, we form our characters. Each time we do a good act when it is difficult, it becomes easier to do a good act next time and – through this development – we become naturally good people. We choose what we are to be like. Even those who suffer at the hands of evil people have choices; they can choose whether to bear their suffering with patience, to understand why other people are acting as they do and to forgive them if they ask, or (alternatively) they can choose to be bitter and unforgiving. Suffering gives sufferers choices, and these choices form their characters.

At what point would you say, 'that's *too much* suffering, *now* free will has come at too high a price'? How many people would have to suffer for free will not to be worth it?

Free will is enormously valuable. If the world can't get very bad, then you have fewer opportunities for making decisions and, therefore, you have less control over what can happen. Perhaps the world could have been arranged so that, for example, it wouldn't be possible for a gangster to kidnap and murder a child, but it might be the case that a gangster could kidnap a child for ten hours. If that was all the evil they could do, many people wouldn't have the chance to make a great difference to the world. For example, nobody could achieve the good of saving the child's life. But, if someone's life as a whole – including the good of their having the choice of how to deal with it – is such that it would have been better if they had not lived, then God can compensate them in the afterlife as He is depicted in Jesus's parable of Lazarus and the rich man.[8]

> In the parable of Lazarus and the rich man, a beggar named Lazarus is starving outside of a rich man's gate. In the afterlife, the rich man is tormented, while Lazarus is offered comfort in heaven.

Can our capacity for decision-making also justify some natural evils?

I think it can, yes. Natural evils are those which are outside of our control, such as natural disasters and diseases. However, if the only evils were those produced by human beings, we would not have nearly so many opportunities for developing our characters. Natural evils like diseases allow us to make all sorts of important decisions. If I'm suffering from a nasty disease, I've got a great character-making opportunity for how I can cope with it; I can choose not to complain, to be grateful for the past and so on. Moreover, my friends and family have an opportunity to do good too: they can choose whether to look after me or abandon me in my illness. All natural evils produce opportunities for choice, which we wouldn't otherwise have. Suppose there were *one* less evil, that has the consequence of there being one less opportunity for good. With that said, your earlier question – of how much we'd need to suffer for suffering to outweigh the good of free will – is an important question to ask. I don't know, exactly, where to draw the line. All I wish to claim is that there is not, in the here and now, too much evil in the world.

How about the suffering of non-human animals? Could God limit their anguish without limiting their opportunities for good?

I don't think so. To understand why, let's consider the suffering that predators cause to their prey. Invertebrates eating other invertebrates is like stars absorbing other stars. I see no reason to believe that animals other than mammals are conscious; non-mammalian brains don't have the parts which our brains have when we're conscious. Still, although it seems clear to me that mammals suffer, the brains of most mammals are significantly different from ours in their sizes and their organization; therefore, it is plausible to suppose that they suffer a lot less than we do.

Some mammals, especially the primates, have brains much like ours and so it is plausible to suppose that they suffer more than the lower mammals, although not as much as we do. These mammals also consciously do many good acts – such as preserving their own lives and the lives of their offspring. Doing this involves taking great trouble to avoid suffering and death. The occurrence of evils which they learn to avoid gives meaning and purpose to their lives, which they would not have if there was no suffering to avoid. Animals may not have free will, but the good they do is sufficient to outweigh the suffering they endure. If they really suffer as much as we do, and yet have no free will, then I think there would be a real difficulty about why God should allow that suffering. Human free will justifies a lot of suffering.

At the beginning of our conversation, you suggested that the question of God's existence may be relevant to how we should live. I wonder, however, whether it matters if we choose to do good over evil. Wouldn't a perfectly good God ensure that we end up in heaven no matter how we act?

God wants everybody to be saved, but God also wants everyone to choose their own future. If somebody persistently chooses to pursue evil, then they'll make themselves wicked through their own choice. Wicked people choose to be unhappy and, in the end, God will let them have their unhappiness. Humans, who have significant free will and moral awareness, must be allowed to choose freely to reject God and all that is good. What does God do with those who choose to reject Him and all that is good? Maybe He keeps them alive and allows them to be unhappy, or perhaps He just eliminates them. Either way, we clearly have an interest in choosing good over evil. We were given the gift of free will in order to allow us to become good people through our own free choices.

Afterthoughts

Religious believers are often stereotyped as being anti-scientific. Believing in God, say their critics, is entirely different to believing in protons and electrons. However, as we have seen, Swinburne's arguments for God are couched in terms of simplicity and probability. These are the same principles that guide us when we're selecting between scientific theories and whether unobservable entities – such as protons and electrons – can be said to exist. This is one of the many appealing aspects of Swinburne's view: that he builds his case for God from the general features of the universe. With this in mind, we can also recognize the nuance of Richard's conclusion. As we have seen, he doesn't think that the existence of the universe, the laws of nature or religious experience *prove* the existence of God with absolute certainty. Instead, he argues that these considerations raise the probability of theism beyond the threshold of being 'more likely than not'.

It's worth reflecting on this point further. For most of us, when we're assessing the likelihood of a hypothesis, we find it difficult to judge whether a belief meets the criteria for being 'probabilistically true'. If we don't think that the God-hypothesis has crossed this threshold, then it's important for us to articulate why. For Swinburne, if the world contained significantly more evil and significantly fewer free creatures, God's existence would be less probable. If life was not tremendously good – and the bad outweighed the good – his conclusion, he says, would be quite different. That's where he draws the line . . . so, what would it take to change your mind?

Questions to consider

1. Could God create an unliftable stone?
2. If God exists, is God inside or outside of time?
3. Do religious experiences increase the likelihood of God's existence?
4. Is theism simpler than atheism?
5. How valuable is human freedom?

Recommended reading

Advanced

Richard Swinburne, *The Coherence of Theism*, 2nd edition (Oxford: Oxford University Press, 2016).

> A challenging academic text in which Swinburne explores God's nature. This is important reading for anybody interested in how we should define God and whether the concept of God is coherent.

Richard Swinburne, *The Existence of God*, 2nd edition (Oxford: Oxford University Press, 2004).

> Building from *The Coherence of Theism*, Swinburne develops his popular and powerful case for God's existence. A modern classic, the book explores the universe's origin and fine-tuned nature, before offering arguments from consciousness, religious experience and morality.

Intermediate

Richard Swinburne, *Are We Bodies or Souls?*, revised edition (Oxford: Oxford University Press, 2023).

> If you want to learn more about Swinburne's views on the soul (and why he thinks the soul is compatible with modern science), then this

is the book for you. According to Swinburne, we *are* our souls and will continue to exist in the afterlife.

Richard Swinburne, *Faith and Reason,* 2nd edition (Oxford: Oxford University Press, 2005).

> Following *The Coherence of Theism* and *The Existence of God*, this is the third in Swinburne's instrumental trilogy on the nature and probability of theism. The book argues that we should participate in religion in order to worship God properly and achieve salvation (for ourselves and others), but that is not to say that all religions are equally deserving of our faith.

Beginner

Richard Swinburne, *Is There a God?*, revised edition (Oxford: Oxford University Press, 2010).

> Aimed at a general audience, this short and accessible book includes Swinburne's best-known arguments for the existence of God. There are no intimidating jargon or formulae in this one; it's the perfect place to start if you're new to the field.

Richard Swinburne, *Was Jesus God?* (Oxford: Oxford University Press, 2008).

> Here, Richard argues that if God exists, we should expect Him to take human form in order to share human suffering and teach us how to live. The life of Jesus, he says, is just the type of life we would expect God to live and, therefore, constitutes probable evidence that Christianity is true.

Chapter Three

Reasonable Faith

William Lane Craig

Introduction

To some people, the phrase 'reasonable faith' seems like an oxymoron. As Mark Twain once quipped, 'Faith is believing what you know ain't so.'[1] Even if we don't go to that extreme, many people think that faith is believing in something in the absence of good evidence. Such an understanding of faith is obviously too simplistic. You have faith in your dentist when you allow him to put his fingers in your mouth and to drill on your teeth, precisely because you *do* have good evidence that he's a competent professional. We routinely place our faith in many persons and things because we have sufficient evidence for believing in them. Our question is where belief in God falls on this scale of reasonability. When Christians declare that they have 'faith in God', is this a matter of *reasonable* faith or not?

In this chapter, we'll be speaking to William Lane Craig, Professor of Philosophy at Houston Christian University. Dr Craig has been ranked as the world's third most influential theologian and tenth most influential philosopher over the past thirty years.[2] As well as being a prolific scholar, his vast catalogue of open-access writing, lectures and high-profile public debates have made him a champion among defenders of the Christian faith. As we shall see, Dr Craig's case for God is forensic, his delivery is charismatic and his conclusions are profound.

The arguments mentioned throughout this chapter – the ontological, cosmological, design and moral arguments – are considered to be among the most powerful reasons for believing in God. As you move through this chapter, I encourage you to wrestle with the premises of Craig's arguments. If you can't reject his premises, then you have to accept his conclusion; if you don't, then perhaps you hold an unreasonable faith of your own.

Home is where the Hick is

As a doctoral student, I hear that you were lucky enough to complete your research at the University of Birmingham under the supervision of John Hick. Did you enjoy your time in England?

My wife Jan and I loved our time in England! We found the people so warm and friendly; it was a wonderful place to live. We lived in a small town called 'Sutton Coldfield', just outside of Birmingham, where we had a little house and spent some very happy years. Studying with Professor Hick was like a dream; he was the doctoral advisor 'that which a greater cannot be conceived'! When I arrived, one of the other graduate students took me aside and said, 'Don't ever expect to be on a first-name basis with Professor Hick.' Then, after six weeks of being there, Hick said to me, 'Let's drop this *Professor* bit. Just call me John.'

> Among British philosophers of religion, it is hard to think of a more celebrated figure than John Hick (1922–2012). Today, Hick's views on religious pluralism and God's goodness are taught all over the world.

From then on, we knew him and his wife as 'John and Hazel'. John was like a father figure to me. They were such ordinary, down-to-earth folks. In fact, one day – when my parents visited from the United States – the Hicks took us for a picnic in the English countryside. We threw down our blanket in a nice green field . . . it was only part way through our sandwiches when we realized that we'd pitched up in a pasture full of cow pies! Still, there we had our picnic. Our time in England with the Hicks was so homely and joyful. It was a great time.

You have spent much of your career in the public eye, teaching people about Christian philosophy and debating prominent atheists. How did you become interested in such things?

What made the difference in my life was becoming a Christian in my late teenage years. I suddenly found myself committed to a worldview with profound philosophical implications: the existence of God, the reality of the soul, the possibility of miracles and so forth. When I entered Christian ministry after finishing my graduate studies, it was with the intention of not merely sharing the good news of the gospel with other people but doing so in the context of offering an intellectual defence of a Christian worldview. In Western society, one of the principal obstacles to belief in God is the widespread perception that Christians are somehow intellectually deficient – we're often caricatured as a bunch of emotional Bible-pounders! I wanted to break down that stereotype and offer convincing reasons for theism. In speaking on university campuses, I soon discovered that whereas a few score people will come out to hear a lecture, thousands will come out to hear a debate. It's become pretty clear to me that debate is the forum for evangelism on our contemporary university campuses. I want to show folks that Christianity can go toe-to-toe with the best that atheism has to offer.

If it was not until your late teenage years that you became a Christian, were you raised as an atheist?

I was raised in a nominally Christian household: my parents were culturally Christian, but they weren't practising. Religion didn't have much of an impact on my life until secondary school when I began to question the meaning and purpose of my existence. It was in that search for answers that I met a Christian girl in my German class who told me about the love of God. I was absolutely stunned. The thought that the Creator of the universe could love *me* was too much to take in! I began to read the New Testament and was immediately captivated by the person of Jesus of Nazareth. There was a wisdom to Jesus's teaching and an authenticity about his life that I found irresistible. Then, after six months of the most intense soul searching that I'd ever been through, I finally yielded my life to Christ and took him as my Saviour and Lord. I committed to live the rest of my earthly existence for him and for his glory.

With the exception of Jesus and the girl from your German class, has anybody else had a significant impact on your thinking?

Undoubtedly, my philosophical hero would be Alvin Plantinga. I consider it an inestimable privilege to be alive and working at the same time as such a giant in the history of philosophy. That our lives and careers should overlap is a tremendous blessing. My esteem for Plantinga would probably be most evident in the fact that if I find myself disagreeing with his arguments, the first thing I do is

> Alvin Plantinga is a leading Christian philosopher. Plantinga is best known for his free will defence (which suggests that free will is worth the price of pain and suffering) and his 'Reformed epistemology' (which claims that it is reasonable to believe in God without any evidence or argument).

look for my mistake! For example, for many years I thought that the <u>modal ontological argument</u> was useless. Plantinga disagreed, so I studied his work and came to the very surprising conclusion that it's actually a really good argument!

> The <u>modal ontological argument</u> states that God is, by definition, 'necessary'. A necessary being is one that, if it's *possible* that it exists, *must* exist. Proponents of the argument believe that God's existence is possible and, therefore, actual.

Something rather than nothing

The question of why there is something (the universe) rather than nothing (no universe) might be the greatest mystery in all of philosophy and science. Do you think that God can offer a solution to this seemingly impenetrable problem?

I certainly do. This question connects to one of my favourite arguments for God's existence: the <u>kalām cosmological argument</u>. The argument is made up of two simple premises. The first premise states that *whatever begins to exist has a cause*; then, the second premise claims that *the universe began to exist*. If you think those two statements are true – and we have good reasons for thinking they are – then you have to accept the conclusion that something caused the universe to begin to exist. On that basis,

> One of the earliest proponents of the <u>kalām cosmological argument</u> was the Islamic philosopher al-Ghāzalī (1058–1111). The word '*kalām*' is used to denote Islamic scholasticism.

you can then undertake a conceptual analysis of what it means to be a cause of the universe, and what you get from that analysis is a number of theologically striking properties. The end result, I think, is that there exists a beginningless, uncaused, timeless, spaceless, immaterial, enormously powerful, personal Creator of the universe.

There are some astrophysicists who claim that the universe *didn't* have a beginning. The universe, they say, is stuck in an infinite loop of big bangs and big crunches. What do you make of this response?

This model of the universe is now out of date. These so-called 'oscillating models' of the universe – in which the cosmos is like an accordion, expanding and contracting from eternity past – were explored back in the 1970s with little success. Not only was it discovered that these theories were physically untenable but, ironically, they implied the very beginning of the universe that they sought to avoid. The reason lies in entropy. Entropy accumulates and is conserved from cycle to cycle. Therefore, if the universe had been oscillating from eternity past, then we should expect our current universe to have a very high entropy level, which would place us in a state of thermodynamic heat death. Obviously, that's not the universe we find

> The second law of thermodynamics, entropy, states that the disorder of a closed system will increase over time. In other words, all *order* (the universe) will turn to *disorder* (a state of heat death). Entropy also offers the best explanation for Matt Damon's career trajectory.

ourselves in. Therefore, cosmologists have largely given up on these models.

Why should we believe that this 'self-existent foundation' is God? Why not say, as Daniel Dennett and Jessica Frazier have argued, that the universe *itself* is the uncaused cause?

The reason is very simple: because the universe began to exist! This fact not only undercuts atheistic worldviews, but any philosophy that says the universe is eternal. We have very good reasons for thinking that the universe had a starting point, which narrows down the scope of the possible explanations of the world to the great monotheistic faiths: Judaism, Islam, Christianity and deism. If the atheist is

> The God of deism is not interested in the world's affairs: God created the universe but, beyond creation, doesn't interact with it.

going to claim that the universe popped into existence out of nothing, as if by magic, then it's clear that theism is a more plausible alternative.

But what makes you think the universe was created by a timeless, spaceless, personal agent? Couldn't the universe have been brought into existence by a physical mechanism?

I've laid out three reasons for thinking that the cause of the universe is a transcendent, unembodied mind. Very briefly summarized, these are as follows. First, the only candidates we know of for a timeless, spaceless, immaterial being are either abstract objects (like numbers) or an unembodied mind; but abstract objects by definition cannot cause anything. Second, the only way to explain the origin of a temporal world with a beginning – from a permanent, eternal cause – is if that cause is a personal agent who can freely choose to create a world in time without any prior determining conditions. Third, causal explanations can either be given in terms of natural laws and initial conditions, or of a personal agent and his volitions; however, an absolutely first physical state of the universe cannot be explained in terms of natural laws and prior conditions. Therefore, the best explanation for why there is something rather than nothing is that the universe was created by a timeless, spaceless, personal being.

And I think to myself, 'what a finely tuned world'

There are critics of theism, such as <u>David Hume</u>, who have argued that the universe could have been created by an 'infantile' or 'senile' god – a god that knows *some* things but not *all* things – rather than the God of Christianity.[3] What do you make of this critique?

The argument from fine-tuning doesn't try to prove that the Designer is omniscient, but simply unfathomably intelligent. So, in response to the argument against the Creator's intelligence, I should appeal to the world's finely tuned parameters. I would say that the degree of fine-tuning that is required for a life-permitting universe is so incomprehensible that the Creator couldn't be some infantile or superannuated deity. Without fine-tuning, not even atomic matter or chemistry would exist – let alone planets, stars and intelligent creatures. Our finely tuned universe cries out for an adequate explanation. The Creator has to be a supremely intelligent mathematician.

> David Hume (1711–1776) was a leading figure of the Scottish Enlightenment. Hume's *Dialogues Concerning Natural Religion* (1779) is one of the most important texts in philosophy of religion. In the *Dialogues*, three characters – who all believe in God – debate God's nature. The book was so controversial for its time that Hume chose not to have it published until after his death.

What kind of odds are we talking about here? Just how finely tuned are the laws of nature?

To take one example, the physicist Sir Roger Penrose calculates that the initial low entropy condition of the universe would have to be fine-tuned to one part in $10^{10(123)}$.[4] That number is so inconceivably large that to call it 'astronomical' would be a wild understatement. I'm not exaggerating when I say we're dealing with incomprehensible numbers and, therefore, an incomprehensibly great intelligence.

As you've said, one day the universe may reach a state of thermodynamic heat death. Some astrophysicists disagree; instead, they believe that the world will end because we're living in a <u>false vacuum</u>. Does the inescapable collapse of the universe not imply a *lack* of design?

Not at all! The thermodynamic properties of the universe, especially its initial low entropy condition, are among the most powerful examples of fine-tuning there is. Without these properties, we wouldn't be having this conversation. It's quite right that we could be hung up in a false vacuum state. But not forever! Unless the universe had a beginning, we would have already tunnelled out of such a state. If the universe were to tunnel into a *true* vacuum state, then this would bring about the end of the world as we know it. A transformation of the laws of nature would sweep across the universe at the speed of light; everything we know would be undone and a new universe would replace ours. This is where physics and theology agree: I understand this transformation of the universe to be a dramatic, scientific analogue for the

We might live in a 'true vacuum' – a universe where our energy field is stable – but according to contemporary physics, this is highly unlikely. In reality, the energy field (our physical laws) may be temporary; in other words, we're probably living in a <u>false vacuum</u>. At any moment, the cosmos could shift from our false vacuum into a true vacuum, destroying everything in our habitable universe including – thank God – the possibility of another *Fast & Furious* movie.

second coming of Christ. We believe that God will eventually roll up the scroll and bring about the end of the universe. Remember that for the theist, this universe is but the cramped and narrow foyer that opens up into the great hall of God's eternity. The end is not the grave, but we shall live forever in personal fellowship with God. On the one hand, it seems crazy to think that the world could come to an end next Tuesday! Yet, this is the position shared by contemporary physicists and Christians alike.

Possible worlds

What do you make of Richard Swinburne's view that the world *could* have existed without God?

I think this is a weakness of his philosophy. Richard does not believe that God exists in every possible world. Instead, he defends the view that God is a contingent being – that God's existence is not logically necessary – and this puts him apart from mainstream Christian thinking. Theologically speaking, his view is terribly deficient. God, a contingent being? The central insight of perfect-being theology and the ontological argument is that God – because He is by definition the greatest conceivable being – must exist necessarily. Even if the ontological argument weren't successful, then God still wouldn't be contingent: God's existence is either necessary or impossible. Contrary to Swinburne, there is no possible world in which God fails to exist and, moreover, no world in which mathematics, logic and moral values can exist independently of God.

It's interesting that you mention moral values. Do you think that we need God in order for moral statements – such as 'helping the needy is good' and 'murdering the innocent is evil' – to be objectively true?

I certainly do. To understand why, let's consider the 'moral argument'. This is another powerful argument for the existence of God that is made up of two straightforward premises. The first premise states that *if God does not exist, then objective moral values and duties do not exist*; then, the second premise claims that *objective moral values and duties do exist*. If you accept both of these premises, then you have to accept the conclusion that God exists.

Not only is this argument simple, but most people don't think there's anything particularly controversial about its premises. Consider the second premise, for example. We're always encountering objective moral values and duties in our everyday lives; moral facts force themselves upon us. Just think about the intrinsic value of other people, for example. Most of us would agree that people are intrinsically valuable: that they should be treated as ends in themselves and not merely as means for some other ends. We think that the Nazi regime was despicably evil and, in contrast, that to sacrifice oneself for another person is morally good. Not only do we recognize these as moral facts, but we take them to be binding independently of whether anyone believes them to be true or not. This is what it means to say that something is 'objectively' good or bad. If somebody were to say that 'the Holocaust was evil', then they would be right; if they were to say that 'the Holocaust was good', then they would be wrong. There is a truth to the matter; it isn't just a matter of opinion. In order for there to be objective moral facts, there needs to be a source of the moral values that we find in the world – that is to say, there has to be a standard, an embodiment of the ultimate good. It is this 'embodiment of the ultimate good', in my view, that we call 'God'.

So, what makes something 'right' or 'wrong' for the atheist?

Well, if atheism is true, then we're just the accidental by-products of the blind evolutionary process. This is the position of Richard Dawkins and Daniel Dennett, for example, who claim that we're nothing more than DNA machines. If this is correct, then moral values are just the offshoots of parental teaching, social conditioning and evolution by natural selection. On atheism, 'good' just means what is 'socially fashionable' or 'evolutionarily beneficial' and 'bad' what is 'socially unfashionable' or 'evolutionarily detrimental'. In other words, the reason you don't harm other people is simply because you don't want them to harm you. There is no objectivity here. However, even diehard atheists such as Dawkins condemn human sacrifice and the religious indoctrination of children. These are objective moral claims. So, almost everybody I have met is convinced that objective moral values exist. On the off chance that you meet somebody who claims to be a moral relativist, just ask them what they think of the traditional Hindu practice of burning widows alive with their husbands. If moral values don't stand independently from what people think, then we can't say that such a practice is wrong. For what it's worth, I don't think views such as <u>pantheism</u> work here either. One of the most horrible features of pantheistic religions is their denial of the absolute distinction between good and evil. According to pantheistic views such as Hinduism, all distinctions – including the distinction between good and evil –

> According to <u>pantheism</u>, God and the universe are identical: God is the universe, and the universe is God.

are illusory. Reality is amoral. I think we should reject such views. There's a fact of the matter when we say that 'genocide is evil' or 'love is good'.

Stephen Law has offered what has become a popular objection to belief in God's goodness. He calls this objection, 'the evil-god challenge'. According to Law, belief in an all-powerful, all-knowing *good* god is no more reasonable than belief in an all-powerful, all-knowing *evil* god and,

therefore, theists are unjustified in favouring belief in one god over the other. How would you respond to this argument?

Let's be careful to understand his argument. Law thinks that it would be ridiculous to believe that there is an evil god. His point is that just as the good in the world refutes the idea of an evil god, so the evil in the world refutes the idea of a good god. Stephen's argument begins from the assumption that theists decide that God is good by analysing the sort of world that God has created. This is a mistake. Christians don't believe in the goodness of God because of an inductive survey of the world – that is, seeing all of the good things that happen, we therefore conclude, 'Wow, God must be really good!' I agree with Stephen entirely: you could not refute the existence of an evil god by pointing to all the good things that happen. Both those arguments are awash. These kinds of speculations – about how much good and evil is in the world – are beyond our ability to make with any real confidence.

In reality, Christians attribute goodness to God – not because the world is good, but – because of facts relating to objective moral values and what it means to be 'God'. Let's consider both of these reasons. First, as we have seen, the moral argument discloses that there needs to be an ontological foundation for the world's objective moral values and duties. Let us suppose, for the sake of argument, that Law's evil god exists. The fact that god is evil implies that He fails to fulfil His moral obligations; but where do these moral obligations come from? Law's evil god couldn't be the 'supreme being': there must be a being who is even higher than evil god, a source of the moral obligations that evil god chooses to rebel against. It is this source of moral obligations that Christians call 'God'.

Second, while the idea of an evil god with a lowercase 'g' is possible, it's metaphysically impossible for God with a capital 'G' to be evil, because God is *by definition* a being which is worthy of worship – God is the 'greatest conceivable being' – and, therefore, God has to be morally good. It would be absurd to say that 'the greatest conceivable being is evil', because it is far greater to be good than it is to be evil. I think we should ground God's goodness in something like the moral argument or the ontological argument, rather than by conducting some inductive survey of the world's goods and evils.

What would you say to those who do not claim to know *how much* evil is in the world but think, nonetheless, that we can rule out God's existence on the basis of the evil that we do know about?

As difficult as the problem of evil and suffering is emotionally, I think it's very difficult to show philosophically or intellectually that it's improbable that God has morally sufficient reasons for permitting evil and suffering to exist. At the risk of oversimplifying, let me just say this: it's not improbable that only in a world suffused with natural and moral suffering would the optimal number of people freely come to know God and find eternal life. Let us not forget that this is a world in which the human drama of redemption is being played out. Given that God's overriding purpose for the world is to bring people freely into His eternal love, I think that justifies the permission of all the world's evils.

'God so loved the world'

So far, we've been discussing God and theism quite broadly; for example, most of the arguments that you have offered could be used in support of the God of Judaism (Yahweh) or Islam (Allāh). As a Christian, however, you face the challenge of justifying your faith in Jesus as part of the Holy Trinity. How do you go about doing this? To take an example, what makes the New Testament more reliable than other holy books, such as the Qur'an which rejects Trinitarian conceptions of God?[5]

According to the doctrine of the Holy Trinity, there is only one God. However, this God exists as three distinct but equally divine persons: the Father, the Son and the Holy Spirit.

The holy book of Islam, the Qur'an, explicitly rejects that Jesus was the incarnation of God. 'Do not speak of a Trinity', it says, 'God is far above having a son.'

Wolfhart Pannenberg (1928–2014) was a prolific systematic theologian who aimed to ground Christianity in objective, knowable facts, such as the historical evidence for Jesus's resurrection.

After I finished my work at the University of Birmingham, I moved to Germany where I completed my second doctorate – this time in theology – under the great Wolfhart Pannenberg. My research focused on the historical credibility of Jesus's resurrection from the dead. What I discovered was that the historical grounds for belief in Jesus's resurrection are far greater than I ever anticipated. Indeed, the central facts underpinning the inference to Jesus's resurrection are agreed upon by the vast majority of New Testament critics. Moreover, I would argue that the best explanation of those facts is the one that the original disciples gave: God raised Jesus from the dead. Therefore, the best conclusion to draw is that God raised Jesus from the dead, thereby authenticating the allegedly 'blasphemous' claims that Jesus made during his life – including his claims to be divine.

Let's contrast this with the records of the Qur'an. The Qur'an was written 600 years after Jesus's death by a man who had no acquaintance with the New Testament; it's a text that was written too late and is too derivative to provide a credible source of information about the historical Jesus. One of the greatest embarrassments for Muslims is that the Qur'an denies the one fact about Jesus which is universally accepted by non-Muslim scholars: that Jesus was executed by Roman crucifixion. The Qur'an says, 'they did not crucify him' and 'they did not kill him', but that Jesus's crucifixion was only an appearance.[6] This view of Jesus is historically indefensible and, therefore, no credible historian turns to the Qur'an as a source of information about Jesus's life.

But do we really have enough evidence to say that 'Jesus rose from the dead'? What would you say to atheists – such as Richard Dawkins, for example[7] – who argue that 'extraordinary claims require extraordinary evidence'?

This slogan, that 'extraordinary claims require extraordinary evidence', is demonstrably false. You don't need to have lots of evidence in order to establish that a highly improbable event has occurred. What probability theorists have come to understand is that we need to ask how likely the evidence would be if the event in question had *not* occurred. In this case, the hypothesis that Jesus was raised from the dead makes the evidence much more probable than any non-miraculous hypothesis. For example, the evidence of the empty tomb, the post-mortem appearances of Jesus and the origin of the Christian faith are vastly more probable given the fact that God raised Jesus from the dead than those facts would be if nothing happened. It's false that in order to establish an extraordinary claim you need to have extraordinary evidence. Dawkins just doesn't understand how the probability calculus works.

Outside of scripture, do you think there are any metaphysical reasons for favouring a Trinitarian conception of God?

Well, here's one argument that you might find interesting. God is by definition 'the greatest conceivable being' and, therefore – as it is greater to be a loving being than not – God must be all-loving. However, it is the very nature of love to give oneself to another. Now who is the other then, to whom God gives His love? Of course, He gives love to humans, but humans have not always existed, and they don't exist in every possible world. Yet, love must be an essential property of God: even when there are no human beings, God must be loving. This means that there must be someone other than humans for God to love, which suggests that the other to whom God gives His love is *internal* to God. So, I think this – while not showing that there are exactly *three* persons in the Godhead – makes it plausible to think that there are multiple persons who are internal to God. This is another advantage that the multi-personal Christian God has over the isolate monad that is Yahweh or Allāh.

In the Qur'an, we're told that Allāh does *not* love some humans. For example, Allāh does not love the sinners and the non-believers. Do you think that Christianity and Islam understand God's love differently?

It's like night and day. In the New Testament, Jesus tells us that 'God so loved the *world*' – and He meant the unbelieving world – 'that He gave His only son, that whoever believes in Him will not perish, but have everlasting life'.[8] In stark contrast, one of the things that struck me as I studied the Qur'an during my doctoral work in Germany was how it says, over and over and over again, like a drumbeat: 'Allāh does not love sinners',[9] 'Allāh does not love unbelievers',[10] 'Allāh does not love the proud',[11] 'Allāh does not love the prodigal'.[12] It struck me so forcefully that according to the Qur'an, Allāh does not love precisely those people that Jesus says God loves so much. Allāh's love is partial and has to be earned. He only loves those who first love Him. I say this publicly in my dialogues and debates with Muslim theologians: I think that Islam has a morally defective concept of God. The God of Islam is *not* all-loving.

Afterthoughts

Many philosophers agree that Craig succeeds in competing with the very best that atheism has to offer. No doubt the simplicity of his arguments is appealing, yet, in my view, these arguments are most praiseworthy because they capture why so many people believe in God in the first place. Prejudice aside, many of us agree that the Big Bang does not explain *why* the universe exists, that the laws of nature are *delicately balanced* and that there is something *objectively* wrong about harming innocent people. Instead of straw-manning theism and claiming that a Christian's faith is blind, we need to focus on these motivations – the best philosophical reasons – for thinking that faith can be reasonable.

An important theme of this chapter is Craig's understanding of God as the embodiment of perfect goodness. The moral argument, which claims that we need God in order for there to be objective moral values, is particularly interesting. If objective moral values don't exist, then there's no *fact* of the matter when somebody says that 'genocide is wrong'. For many, this is too bitter of a pill to swallow. The alternative, however, looks just as unappealing. Suppose, for example, that the atheist declares they *do* believe in objective moral values. The problem with this approach is that atheists are typically naturalists – that is, they only believe in natural properties (protons and neutrons) and laws (gravity and motion) – but if the only things that exist are that which we find in nature, then *where are* the objective moral values? It's not like we find laws of logic and morality swinging from trees and sprouting from the ground! Objective values are a very different type of thing. Perhaps Craig is right; if we believe in objective moral values, maybe we need to believe in something supernatural.

Questions to consider

1. Does God provide the best explanation for the existence of the universe?
2. If God exists, would God have to be a supremely intelligent mathematician?
3. How do objective moral values instil themselves in us?
4. Do extraordinary claims require extraordinary evidence?
5. Would an all-loving God have to be multi-personal?

Recommended reading

Advanced

William Lane Craig, *Atonement and the Death of Christ: An Exegetical, Historical, and Philosophical Exploration* (Waco, TX: Baylor University Press, 2020).

> If you're looking for a deep dive into the nature and significance of Jesus's death and resurrection – Christianity's central doctrine – then Craig's thorough, interdisciplinary *Atonement and the Death of Christ* has you covered.

William Lane Craig, *The Kalām Cosmological Argument* (Eugene, OR: Wipf and Stock Publishers, 1979).

> This is Craig's first ground-breaking book, in which he develops and defends what is now one of the most popular arguments for God's existence: the *kalām* cosmological argument. The themes covered throughout the book include the nature of infinity, the beginning of time and the destiny of the universe.

Intermediate

William Lane Craig, *Reasonable Faith: Christian Truth and Apologetics*, third edition (Wheaton, IL: Crossway Books, 2008).

> Here you'll find all of Craig's best arguments in one place. As ever, Craig makes his case for God with remarkable clarity and detail. The book can be read from beginning to end, or you can just pick out sections that grab your interest. Craig's second chapter, on the absurdity of life without God, comes highly recommended.

Katie Mack, *The End of Everything (Astrophysically Speaking)* (London: Penguin Books, 2020).

> If you enjoyed our discussion of how the universe will end, then this is an absolute must-read. In this popular, entertaining and accessible book, astrophysicist Katie Mack explores the predominant theories of the end times and their existential implications.

Beginner

William Lane Craig and Joseph E. Gorra, *A Reasonable Response: Answers to Tough Questions on God, Christianity, and the Bible* (Chicago, IL: Moody Publishers, 2013).

> This book is packed with deep and profound questions on a whole range of topics, including epistemology, morality, God, the meaning of life, evil and the afterlife. Whenever you're introduced to a new area of Christian philosophy, it's always worth dipping into this book to hear Craig's thoughts on the matter.

William Lane Craig, *On Guard: Defending Your Faith With Reason and Precision*, student edition (Colorado Springs, CO: David C. Cook, 2010).

> If you're brand new to philosophy of religion and Craig's work, then this book is an excellent place to start. *On Guard*, with its informal and personal prose, defends four arguments for God's existence. The book is written for Christians, but it makes for an excellent introduction for anybody who is newly interested in the field.

Chapter Four

The Necessary Existent

Mohammad Saleh Zarepour

Introduction

What grounds existence? What is the entity, if any, upon which the cosmos depends? As Craig explained in our previous chapter, the mainstream view among Abrahamic believers is that the world requires a self-existent cause: a God who couldn't fail to exist. Theists often arrive at this conclusion by appealing to their senses: considerations of morality, fine-tuning and causation. The issue with relying on our senses, however, is that they're fallible; after all, we can't be *certain* that the world exists in the way it appears. If we want *absolute* knowledge of God, then we need a different method of proof.

In this chapter, we'll be discussing Islamic metaphysics with Mohammad Saleh Zarepour. Zarepour is one of the world's leading experts on Avicennian philosophy, according to which we can prove God's existence from the concept of existence alone. For <u>Avicenna</u> – one of Zarepour's intellectual heroes – we can deduce God's existence from a simple starting point: that something exists. That something could be anything – a sock, a star, a stone – but its existence requires an explanation.

<u>Avicenna</u> (980–1037) – or *Ibn Sīnā* – made important contributions to various disciplines, from philosophy to medicine. Engaging with the intellectual heritage of Aristotle (384–322 BCE), Avicenna introduced a series of original ideas that would inspire generations of thinkers, not only from the Islamic tradition but also Christianity (such as Aquinas) and Judaism (such as Maimonides).

The thesis of this chapter is that we can arrive at Allāh's existence – and all of Allāh's attributes – simply by reflecting on the idea of a 'necessary existent'. What emerges from this is a world in which Allāh, like the God of the Bible, is invested in the world's creation and divine justice. Still, there

are important differences between Islam and Christianity – differences with significant philosophical implications. It is these differences, says Zarepour, that give Muslims the advantage over their Abrahamic cousins.

The wise one

Before we discuss the nature of God, I wonder what you think about the nature of philosophy more generally. In your view, what *is* philosophy?

I see philosophy as an argument-oriented discipline that aims to discuss fundamental questions about the ultimate nature of things, how (if at all) we can gain knowledge and how (and why) we should live. There are even words within that definition that need discussing. For example, when we're talking about an 'argument', we need to understand what the word 'argument' means; similarly, when I say the 'fundamental questions about nature of things', you need to know what I mean by 'fundamental', 'nature' and 'things'. Ironically, these are themselves among the questions that philosophers try to answer. Nevertheless, what I said captures what philosophy is, or so it seems to me.

What do you make of Richard Dawkins's view that philosophy is about getting clear on the questions before passing them on to science, where the 'real progress' is made?

I think that's wrong. The very question of whether there is anything inaccessible to science is a significant philosophical question which can't be answered by science. Moreover, there are lots of other issues that are inaccessible to science. To take some examples: what does it mean to possess *consciousness*? Do *numbers* exist? What makes a *good* or *bad* person? These aren't questions that science can answer, and we shouldn't pretend it can. I mean, how would science even begin to tell us how we can make our lives or societies *virtuous*, to put it in Socratic language. The same is true for questions of metaphysics and God. Personally, I'm interested in such fundamental questions; and philosophers have made great progress with some of these questions. It must be noted that the progress of philosophy shouldn't be evaluated based on the same criteria as the progress of science. However, this is a distinct issue that must be postponed to another discussion.

> Metaphysics is the study of ultimate reality. Put broadly, it asks what things exist, how existing things relate to each other and why anybody thought *Ocean's Thirteen* (2007) was a good idea.

How did you become interested in questions of God and the world's nature?

My interest in metaphysics and God was inspired by two things. First, I grew up in a Muslim household, so I was introduced to religious education at an early age. Through this education, I began, quite naturally, to start thinking about God's nature. Second, my high school placed a strong emphasis on the importance of critical thinking. In my teenage years – when I was learning about reason, religion, rationality and revelation – questions of God were interwoven with questions of reality.

Thinking back, I suppose I had some pretty strong religious beliefs and wanted to see if they were plausible; that was my main motivation for studying philosophy. In those early years, especially in my mid-twenties, I was very sceptical about whether belief in God could be justified through philosophical arguments. I was never a full-blown atheist, but I certainly doubted the rationality of theism. Over time, however, I came to realize that I was wrong: there is a huge capacity for arguments justifying belief in God.

In academic journals, it seems that publications on Islamic philosophy of religion are quite rare. Do you think that philosophy of religion has a diversity problem?

Certainly, the field is excessively Christianity-oriented. However, the good news is that philosophers are well aware of this problem and are working hard to fix it – and it's a problem worth fixing! After all, engaging with different perspectives doesn't just broaden our own horizons, but it furthers our collective understanding of the reality that we're all trying to understand. There are, however, those who claim that there's no need to diversify – 'There is enough overlap,' they say, 'between the different religious traditions.' I don't think that's right. First, this critique fails to acknowledge that Hinduism, and the other Eastern traditions, are radically different to the Abrahamic faiths. Second, there are even important differences between Judaism, Christianity and Islam. When we ignore these differences, we're not only failing to understand different religions, but we're missing out on the wisdom of our neighbours. There is much to be gained from other religions, and it's about time philosophy of religion woke up to this fact.

The first one

Like any other religion, Islam is a diverse worldview that encompasses a range of different principles and practices. Are there any beliefs within Islam that are considered *essential*?

There are various essential beliefs across the different schools of Islam. However, I would say that the most fundamental premise of Islam is *tawḥīd*. *Tawḥīd* refers to the idea that there is one God and that this God is the ultimate ground of everything. As well as being an explicit denial of polytheism, accepting *tawḥīd* is to say something about God's unity – His *oneness* – which is understood by some Muslim thinkers as implying not only that God is unique but also that God is metaphysically simple. There are many other ideas that fall out of *tawḥīd*, such as

> The word 'Islam' means 'total submission to God'.

> Unlike monotheism, which claims that exactly one God exists, polytheism involves belief in two or more gods.

the implication that everything is under Allāh's control, that everything goes back to Allāh and that, compared to other entities or objects, there is nothing that can rival Allāh's importance.

How does the prophet Muhammad come into this? Does *tawḥīd* also refer to the idea that Muhammad is Allāh's messenger?

Tawḥīd is only about Allāh and His role in the world. However, that doesn't mean that to believe in Islam as a religion is just about believing in God. In my view, the true meaning of *tawḥīd* is something that people across the many different religions have already accepted; belief in one God who grounds everything isn't exclusive to Islam.

> In 610, the angel Gabriel (*Jibrīl*) appeared to Muhammad (c. 570–632) in a cave near Mecca. Gabriel instructed Muhammad to recite verses that were to be included in the Qur'an. Muhammad began to preach about these revelations in public, claiming that people must submit to the 'one true God' and that Muhammad was His messenger.

When you say that Allāh is the 'ultimate ground of everything', what do you mean exactly?

I would like to approach this question through the work of Avicenna, though I'm aware that some Muslims don't like such an approach. Avicenna is probably the most important Islamic thinker in the history of philosophy; he was a polymath, making groundbreaking discoveries across many different disciplines. With a touch of exaggeration, we may say that Avicenna was the philosopher who got Muslims to forget about Aristotle. He wasn't intimidated by any authority; he was a profound, innovative thinker who drew heavily from the philosophical tradition he inherited but by no means confined himself to it. According to Avicenna, all of the properties usually attributed to God can be extracted from the concept of a 'necessary existent'. A necessary existent cannot fail to exist and, therefore, a necessary existent cannot *not* exist. But Avicenna shows us that there is only one necessary existent. God is *the* necessary existent and the ultimate ground of everything else.

> The philosophy of Aristotle (384–322 BCE) continues to influence modern philosophy and science; his work dominated European thought from his death until the Renaissance (fourteenth–seventeenth century).

The obvious question is why we should think there's a necessary existent in the first place. I'm a contingent existent – I depend on oxygen, coffee and my parents meeting on that fateful day. Why can't we just have an infinite series of contingent things?

To address this concern, Avicenna introduced his famous 'proof of the sincere'. Think of it like this: things are either contingent, impossible or necessary. That's a very straightforward distinction; everything has to fall into one of these three categories. Some things are contingent, meaning that they *could* come into existence. (Of course, contingent things can also go *out* of existence.) To take an example, your children might not exist, but you could decide to bring them into reality. That's what it means for something to be contingent: it's *neutral* with respect to existence and non-existence. To upset this neutrality, there must be something to make one side heavier – something to tip the scales and cause that contingent to exist rather than not exist, or not exist rather than exist. In other words, every contingent thing requires a cause.

> Avicenna's *burhān al-ṣiddīqīn* – which translates to something like 'the proof of the sincere' or 'the demonstration of the truthful' – aims to establish the existence of God as the necessary existent. It has been argued that, like the ontological argument, the proof of the sincere does not rely on observations of the world. Instead, the argument claims to prove God's existence by reflecting on the nature of existence itself. That is how, Avicenna believes, the most sincere people prove the existence of God: through reflection upon His own nature, which is necessary existence, not through reflection upon His creatures.

Now, we all accept that *something* exists; after all, we can't deny our own existence. Therefore, the question is this: is this 'something' contingent or necessary? If it's necessary, then we have what we want: a necessary existent. However, if it's contingent, that 'something' must have been caused by something else; after all, that's what it means to be contingent. Your question was whether we could have an infinite series of contingent things. According to Avicenna, even if we accept an endless chain of causally connected beings, you can still talk about 'the totality of all contingent beings' in the world. Then, we can ask whether this totality is itself contingent or necessary. If you say that it's necessary, then we have a necessary existent. However, if you say that it's contingent, then it must have a cause. This cause must be external to the totality because part of a thing cannot cause the whole thing; so, the cause of the totality of all contingent beings must be external to this totality. Therefore, it cannot be a contingent being; it must be a necessary existent, and this proves that there is a necessary existent.

The only one

So, no matter how we look at it, we always end up with a necessary existent. This is still very far away from the God of Islam, however, who is said to be all-loving, all-knowing and all-powerful. Why can't atheists, for example, just say that the *universe* is the necessary existent?

The argument we've discussed doesn't have any problem with the claim that the universe is necessary. This shows that Avicenna's argument is actually very powerful; if Judaism, Christianity, Hinduism and even atheism can agree that there's a necessary existent *somewhere*, then that's to Avicenna's credit.

It's worth mentioning that Avicenna does have an argument for favouring God over atheism. Avicenna's proof begins by showing that there cannot be more than one necessary existent. Let's assume that's true for the moment. Now, if there is just one necessary existent, the question is whether it has parts or no parts. If it has parts, then those parts must be necessary or contingent. They can't be contingent, however, because if the parts of the necessary existent were contingent, then the whole thing would be contingent; in that case, the parts must be necessary. Yet, if these parts were necessary, then we have something with at least two necessary parts: but this contradicts our earlier assumption that there is only one necessary thing. It follows that the necessary existent must be metaphysically simple: having

> Unlike the necessary existent, Tabasco's Original Red Pepper Sauce® is made up of three simple ingredients: salt, peppers and vinegar. Tabasco is best combined with tar water.

no parts. The universe has many parts – trees, trains, toddlers, Tabasco – and, therefore, the argument concludes, the universe can't *be* the necessary existent.

That's a fascinating argument, but what reason does Avicenna give for the uniqueness of the necessary existent? Why can't we have more than one necessary thing?

There are good philosophical reasons for this. For there to be more than one necessary existent, there would have to be something that makes these multiple necessary existents different from one another. After all, if there was nothing different about them, these necessary existents would be identical. Therefore, there must be an individuating factor. The question is whether the individuating factor of a necessary existent would be *essential* to it or something *accidental* – that is, something that is added to its essence. It can't be *essential* to it because that would make the two necessary existents identical; they would be of the same essence. Yet, the individuating factor of a necessary existent could not be an accident – or a non-essential property – added to its essence, otherwise, the additional property must be made by something other than the necessary existent in question. This makes that necessary existent dependent on that *other* thing. So, it would be – at least partially – caused by something else. But a necessary existent cannot be caused at all, otherwise, it would be by definition a contingent existent. Therefore, there can only be one necessary existent.

This takes us back to Islam's fundamental premise, *Tawḥīd*: God's uniqueness. This belief is so central to Islam that, according to the Qur'an, saying that there are multiple Gods – and not just Allāh – is the only sin that Allāh will never forgive![1]

A similar argument is offered by the philosopher <u>Moses Mendelsohn,</u> who writes, 'I am, therefore there is a God.'[2] In other words, if at least one thing exists, then there must be a necessary existent.

If 'God' is understood as 'the necessary existent', then Mendelsohn's approach would be very similar to Avicenna's; however, I think we can go a step further. In an Avicennian framework, there only needs to be the *possibility* that something exists; we don't even need to claim that something *does* exist. According to the Proof of the Sincere, the existence of something – whatever it is – implies the existence of a necessary existent. As a result, the *possibility* of the existence of something implies the *possibility* of the existence of a necessary existent. However, the possibility of the existence of a necessary existent is tantamount to the *existence* of a necessary existent.[3] In other words, the mere possibility of the existence of something implies the existence of the necessary existent. That's the beauty of the Avicennian approach. From our armchairs, we can conclude that if *anything* is possible, then there must be a necessary, unique, uncaused, simple, self-subsisting, self-independent entity that grounds all of reality. As Muslims, we call this being 'Allāh'.

> <u>Moses Mendelsohn</u> (1729–1786) was a central figure of the Jewish Enlightenment (the *Haskalah*). Mendelssohn argued that Judaism was not a religion of dogma but a set of natural truths accessible to everyone. He tried to show this by offering several *self-evident* proofs of the existence of God.

The just one

In addition to these attributes, Allāh is also said to have <u>ninety-nine names</u> – from 'the wise one' to 'the just one'. Does Avicenna give reasons for attributing these other qualities to Allāh?

Avicenna did not discuss all these attributes in detail, but he seems to believe that all such attributes can in principle be extracted from God as the necessary existent. He demonstrated this for some of the most important attributes of God. I'll discuss a few of them. Every material being is composed of parts; therefore – because the necessary existent is not composed of parts – Allāh must be immaterial. Appealing to some

> The <u>ninety-nine names</u> of Allāh are those which appear in the Qur'an and *ḥadīth*. Examples include 'the accountant', 'the rich' and 'the bringer of death'.

Neoplatonic ideas – whose details cannot be expanded here – Avicenna shows that everything immaterial is intelligible. Moreover, everything intelligible which does not subsist in matter or another intellect, must itself be an intellect. Therefore, the necessary existent – as a purely immaterial being that does not subsist in anything else – is a pure intellect. To discuss another example, Avicenna claims that goodness is 'pure existence'. In contrast, evil is the absence of existence: evil is privation of Being or goodness. God is the source and cause of the existence of everything. Therefore, God is the source of all the goodness in the world. Moreover, enjoying the ideal form of existence – that is, the Necessary Existence – God possesses the ideal form of goodness. God is all good and the source of everything good in the universe.

> The term 'Neoplatonic' refers to the school of thought that emerged in the third century whose ideas were based on interpretations of Plato (c. 428–348 BCE).

> According to the privation theory of evil, evil is nothing more than an absence, or a lack, of form or goodness. For example, illness is the absence of health, poverty is the absence of wealth and Adam Sandler is the absence of talent.

According to mainstream Islamic traditions, hell is a real place where evil-doers and non-believers are punished for eternity. There are many critics of this view. For example, Susan Blackmore has argued that scaring children with 'sores, boiling water, peeling skin, burning flesh, dissolving bowels and an everlasting fire that burns you forever' is morally indefensible. Does hell not show that Allāh is *not* perfectly good?

If we are to talk about Islamic conceptions of hell, we need to discuss all of the statements about heaven (*jannah*) and hell (*jahannam*) in the Qur'an, everything that's contained in the *ḥadīth* and all of the interpretations of these statements throughout history. Without having these things on the table, we can't say what 'Islam teaches about heaven and hell'. What I can say, however, is that there are Muslim thinkers who claim that eventually hell will be empty.[4] Furthermore, there are interpretations of religious texts that say hell is nothing but the incarnation of our past actions – a place where we're not punished by Allāh but our past selves.[5]

> A *ḥadīth* (Arabic plural *aḥādīth*) – meaning 'account' or 'narrative' – is a report about Muhammad's words, actions and teachings. In English, '*the ḥadīth*' usually refers to such reports in a collective way.

On this account, what we receive in the afterlife isn't some further, external thing that's imposed on us by Allāh; hell is just the true nature of our actions coming back to us.

If you're ever looking for an alternative career, Saleh, you'd make a fantastic politician! Can I push you on this? Do *you* believe in traditional ideas of heaven and hell?

I would like to address this question through Theodore Sider's puzzle of hell.[6] The puzzle begins by acknowledging that heaven and hell are two extremely different places: one of them is extremely good and the other is extremely bad. Significantly, God has to decide on a threshold, a 'cut-off point' where some people *just about* go to heaven and some people *just about* go to hell. That means there's going to be people who are very close to the cut-off point, morally speaking, but are rewarded with extreme happiness or extreme suffering. That doesn't look like justice to me, and, therefore, I don't think God – 'the just one' – will create a system like this. My intuition is that justice ought to be proportional, ruling out the binary conception of heaven and hell across the major world religions. I say this in a very non-political way: this binary conception of heaven and hell *must* be rejected.

On the traditional view, what does the afterlife look like? Is it a physical place?

According to a literal interpretation of the Qur'an, the afterlife will involve a bodily resurrection. We know, at least from works in contemporary philosophy of religion, that this idea can be defended.[7] Interestingly, Avicenna thought that bodily resurrection was impossible – he wasn't convinced by any of the philosophical arguments for a physical afterlife. Instead, he accepted physical resurrection on the grounds of revelation. With that said, Avicenna's philosophy can be used to motivate a range of eschatological views. For example, he believes that the body is not an essential component of the soul. Therefore, regardless of whether or not bodily resurrection is possible, the soul

> Eschatology studies the world's end or the end of human life. A complete eschatological theory will explain how and why the universe will end, and what does (or does not) await us after death.

can – and, in fact, does – continue to exist after the death of the body.

How can we show that the body and the soul are two separate things?

Avicenna argues for this claim through his 'floating man argument', which is also sometimes referred to as 'the flying man argument'. This is probably one of the most famous thought experiments in the history of philosophy.[8] The argument goes like this. Imagine that you are created out of thin air: you don't feel the weight of your body, you can't feel your skin, you can't see, hear, smell or taste, and you don't have memories of the past. In other words, you have no access to the external world. You're just floating about in the cosmos; you can't even feel your thin-air-made body. Given these conditions, Avicenna asks whether you could know that you exist. His answer is positive: even if we don't know anything about our own body, let alone the external world, we can still say that we exist. We all have some form of self-awareness. But if it is possible to have self-awareness without being aware of our body, then our self (or soul) should be distinct from our body. The floating man is aware of himself without being aware of his body and, therefore, his soul is separate from his body. If this is true, then the soul can in principle survive the death of the body. Admittedly, this formulation of the floating man argument is objectionable. Nevertheless, I think some more precise formulations of this argument can support the idea of the separateness of the body from the soul.

Some philosophers, such as William Lane Craig, speak quite damningly about Allāh's moral character. For example, Craig portrays Allāh as a spiteful deity who 'only loves those who first love Him'. In fact, he goes as far as to say that Islam has a 'morally defective' idea of God. What do you make of Craig's assessment?

I couldn't disagree more. For a start, Craig's reading of the Qur'an isn't accurate. When discussing the God of Islam, we need to consider *all* of the relevant Qur'anic verses; you can't just cherry-pick them. If Craig looked at the Qur'an more holistically, he'd reach a very different conclusion about Allāh.

For Christians, benevolence and forgiveness seem to be God's most important attributes. In the Qur'an, however, the emphasis isn't just on God's love but on a group of attributes that should be considered as a collective. For example, God isn't *just* love but *also* power and justice. When we combine these concepts, we see that Allāh has a different relationship with His people than the Christian God does. Justice, power, love – if you only focus on one of Allāh's attributes, you'll end up with some pretty misleading views about Islam.

If God's love is less important within Islam than Christianity, does this give Muslims a slight advantage in responding to the problem of evil?

I think it does, yes. The problem of evil is a serious objection to Christianity; if God is, beyond anything else, *all-loving*, then why is there so much suffering in the world? The existence of evil is incompatible with the biblical God and, therefore, makes the problem more challenging for Christians than it is for Muslims. In the Qur'an, we have a very complex picture of God in which love, justice, punishment, reward and all of God's other attributes work in unison. For example, sometimes evil is a punishment, and punishments are just, because God is just. These explanations aren't available to the New Testament Christian who wants to defend an all-loving, all-forgiving father figure with little interest in notions of power and justice.

Craig also rejects Islam because it disregards the evidence for Jesus's crucifixion. What do you make of his case for Jesus's divinity?

There is an excellent paper by Zein Ali in which he offers responses to Craig's claims in this regard.[9] I encourage everyone curious to know whether Craig's views are defensible to read that paper. It is true that, according to the Qur'an, Jesus is not God or the son of God – 'God is far above having a son'[10] – but this does not mean that there is no interpretation of Christianity which is compatible with this understanding of Jesus.

There are <u>anti-theists</u>, however, who argue that Islam doesn't just face the problem of evil but *increases* the amount of suffering in the world. For example, Susan Blackmore and Richard Dawkins have criticized Islam for treating women as second-class citizens. Do you think that Islam has a bigger problem with sexism and misogyny than the other world religions?

According to <u>anti-theists</u>, religion is responsible for more harm than good; proponents typically claim that religion causes fear and conflict. Alternatively, anti-theism may also refer to the *hope* that God doesn't exist; after all, you might not like the idea of God listening to your thoughts or sending you to hell!

I don't think Islam has a bigger problem with prejudice than any other religion. However, there are *interpretations* of Islam in which women are treated worse than they are in other versions of Islam or other faiths. I don't think that any of those misogynist interpretations are plausible. If a Muslim interprets something to be contrary to reason or morality, then it has no place in Islam. Of course, we should be careful not to rely on oversimplified pictures of rationality and morality on which anything one doesn't like could be rendered as being irrational or immoral. However, I believe that according to any acceptable account of rationality and morality, sexism and misogyny are immoral and irrational. We should reject any worldview that says otherwise.

Afterthoughts

There'll be very few philosophers who won't accept the conclusion of Avicenna's proof of the sincere. That's the beauty of his argument: its modesty and ability to find common ground between otherwise diverse worldviews. Identifying the necessary existent is the foundation of almost any coherent metaphysics. Of course, there will be those who are sceptical about our ability to conclude something about the world's nature through *pure* reasoning. 'How arrogant philosophers must be to think they can learn about the origin of the universe without doing any science.' One may have sympathy for this view, yet it does not tell us where Avicenna goes wrong. If his opponents want to criticize his philosophy, then they'll have to do some philosophy.

Of course, more substantial problems arise when we attribute other qualities to the necessary existent. For instance, no sensible philosopher will accept the privation theory of evil – the idea that evil isn't a substance but a lack of substance.[11] The problem is, there's no *lack* when it comes to a nauseating rash or a jellyfish sting: a *lack* of substance would make the thing better, not worse. Without its more controversial premises, one might think that Avicenna's argument doesn't get us very far.

Finally, it's important to reflect on Zarepour's understanding of God's attributes; 'Allāh's being all-loving is neither beyond nor prior to Allāh's other attributes', he says. This raises questions about what it means to be 'the greatest possible being' – Hill's definition of God from our opening chapter. Is a being greater if they prioritize forgiveness and love over everything else, or would God be more worthy of worship if She possesses a range of attributes that are equally important? In the next chapter, Susan Blackmore tells us that it doesn't really matter. Believing in either God, she argues, is as ridiculous as it is dangerous.

Questions to consider

1. If *something* is possible, is that proof of the necessary existent?
2. Could there be more than one necessary existent?
3. What can the 'floating man argument' teach us about personal identity?
4. If you were on the cusp of heaven, would it be wrong for Allāh to send you to hell?
5. Does the existence of evil threaten Christianity more than Islam?

Recommended reading

Advanced

Mohammad Saleh Zarepour, *Necessary Existence and Monotheism: An Avicennian Account of the Islamic Conception of Divine Unity* (Cambridge: Cambridge University Press, 2022).

> In this short academic book, Zarepour makes his case for the necessary existent. In terms of analytic texts on Avicenna's arguments for monotheism and God's unity, this is as good as it gets. Professional philosophers will take a lot from this book, especially if they enjoyed this chapter.

Islamic Philosophy of Religion: Essays from Analytic Perspectives, ed. Mohammad Saleh Zarepour (London: Routledge, 2023).

> This collection includes essays on a diverse range of philosophical issues about Islam. They are all written from analytic perspectives and address topics like the arguments for the existence and uniqueness of God, the attributes of God, miracles, the problem of evil, the problem of divine hiddenness and the relation between science and Islam.

Intermediate

The Oxford Handbook of Islamic Philosophy, ed. Khaled El-Rouayheb and Sabine Schmidtke (Oxford: Oxford University Press, 2017).

> This is a collection of thirty essays on Islamic philosophy. The book manages to cover scholarship from the ninth century to the twentieth, offering detailed expositions and analyses of the most important figures and works in the history of Islamic philosophical thought.[12]

Jon McGinnis, *Avicenna* (Oxford: Oxford University Press, 2010).

> McGinnis's introduction is essential reading for anybody who is interested in learning about Avicenna's wider intellectual activity. The book offers a detailed and accessible guide to Avicenna's approach to psychology and metaphysics, as well as his place, influence and legacy within the history of philosophy and science.

<u>Beginner</u>

Zein Ali, 'Some Reflections on William Lane Craig's Critique of Islam', *The Heythrop Journal*, vol. 60, no. 3 (2019): 397–412.

> This is the article that Zarepour referenced in our interview, in which Ali sets out and responds to Craig's claim that Islam misrepresents the life and person of Jesus. This short and accessible paper also addresses some of Craig's other arguments against Islam, including his contention that the Qur'an fails to understand the Trinity and his evaluation of Allāh's moral character.

Peter Adamson, *Ibn Sīnā (Avicenna): A Very Short Introduction* (New York: Oxford University Press, 2023).

> For those who are completely new to Islamic philosophy and the work of Avicenna, you won't find a better guide than Peter Adamson. This is one of Adamson's shorter books, which gives a 'whirlwind tour' of the life, lessons and legacy of Avicenna and his work. Adamson has published an equally accessible guide to Islamic philosophy – *Philosophy in the Islamic World: A Very Short Introduction*[13] – as part of the same series.

Chapter Five

God Is a Meme

Susan Blackmore

Introduction

Many people have faith in God. They might defend this faith through philosophical arguments, but they don't discover God through philosophy. Religious beliefs aren't formed in a vacuum; ninety-nine per cent of the time, they're accidents of birthplace.[1] If you're born in Israel, you'll believe in Yahweh; for those in Saudi Arabia, it's Allāh; and, in Ancient Greece, it would be Zeus. There's a story to be told here; it's a story about how ideas are formed and their impact on the wider world. The sciences – evolutionary psychology, biology, anthropology and sociology –

> Yahweh (or 'YHWH') is the Hebrew name for God. For many Jews, 'Yahweh' is so sacred that His name should never be spoken aloud.

have a lot to say about the evolution, transmission and survival of these ideas. It is these perspectives to which we now turn our attention.

This chapter features a captivating, original essay from one of the world's leading psychologists, Susan Blackmore. Blackmore began her career exploring the paranormal. In 1970, she had an extraordinary, life-changing out-of-body experience.[2] It convinced her that consciousness extends beyond the body, that

> An out-of-body experience is defined as an experience in which people claim to see the world from a location outside of their physical bodies. Blackmore's experience involved flying through the world and a mystical state of unity with the cosmos.

there's truth to <u>psychokinesis</u> and <u>precognitive dreams</u>, and that life may continue after death. However, after completing her PhD research – in which she conducted an extensive series of experiments on paranormal claims – she came to understand experiences like her own not as evidence for the paranormal, but as important information about the nature of consciousness and the illusions we live with. Today, Blackmore is known for

> The ability to manipulate the physical world with one's mind – without using one's body – is known as '<u>psychokinesis</u>'.

> During <u>precognitive dreams</u>, people are said to experience events that will occur in the future.

opposing the view she once defended: she is a sceptic, an atheist and, as we shall see, she doesn't suffer religion gladly.

This chapter is all about memes. In 1976, Richard Dawkins coined the term '<u>meme</u>' in his multi-million bestseller, *The Selfish Gene*. Dawkins wasn't referring to comically captioned images of SpongeBob SquarePants and Ainsley Harriott. Memes are, in essence, information: they're ideas, concepts, jingles and jokes that exist within our brains and are passed on from person to person. Just as your genes seek to replicate themselves through procreation, memes reproduce themselves through imitation. Today alone, you will have been exposed to a countless number of memes: the tune to Big Yellow Taxi, the benefits of birth control, that Rodger makes the perfect

> The word '<u>meme</u>' is an abbreviation of the Greek term 'mimeme' (meaning 'something imitated'), which is intended to sound like the word 'gene' (the fundamental, underlying, biological code that is subjected to natural selection). According to Dawkins and Blackmore, genes and memes are real entities that *use* us for their own survival.

coffee. These memes are transferred from one person to another, and the memes with the best survival values are passed across cultures and down through the generations. Like your genes, memes don't care. They can't care; like bacteria, viruses and Adam Sandler's movies, their only goal is to replicate.

For Blackmore, one of the leading scholars in <u>memetics</u>, God is just that: a meme. God is not the super-powerful creator of the universe, but the super-powerful *idea* that has evolved over thousands of years. This idea has become tangled up in numerous religious <u>memeplexes</u>, shapeshifting in form to aid its own survival and using us human meme machines for its own propagation. God, says Blackmore, is one of the nastiest and most powerful memes that has ever evolved.[3]

> The study of memes is called '<u>memetics</u>'. Memetics aims to identify and trace different memes, as well as how these memes are replicated. At its core, memetics explores the evolution of human culture.

> Some memes are more likely to survive together than alone. These groups of co-adapted memes – memes that come together for mutual advantage – are referred to as '<u>memeplexes</u>'.

Gods evolving

There is no God who created the universe, no God who made us in His own image, no God who answers (some people's) prayers. There is no all-knowing, all-powerful, supernatural Being who cares about us. There is no creator who has a plan for His Wonderful World and who will rescue us from the mess we are making of it. Yet, even today, roughly four billion people believe in some version of God, many obeying His arbitrary and cruel laws and passing on their false beliefs and restrictive practices to their children. These powerful religious memes tie them to the biology of procreation while the rest of culture speeds away from biology with ideas of sexual and racial equality, freedom, individual happiness and universal human rights. All these freedoms are <u>anathema</u> to the God meme.

> An <u>anathema</u> is something that's cursed or denounced by a religious institution, such as contraception or homosexuality. It may also refer to persons who are condemned or excommunicated, such as Elizabeth I (1533–1603) and Galileo Galilei (1564–1642).

How did this blatantly false idea of God appear, become so powerful and last so long? Evolutionary psychology rejects memetics but can help us understand why our minds evolved to be so vulnerable to religion. For hunter-gatherers, it might have been adaptive for survival to mistake rustling leaves for someone lurking in the undergrowth, rather than miss an enemy or predator. With our evolved ability to understand other people's minds, we willingly attribute intentions, desires, thoughts and emotions to rocks, springs, mushrooms and trees. We can easily imagine 'minimally counter-intuitive' entities and so conjure up invisible tree spirits that think and feel like us, or angels that resemble humans with added wings.

> People may be willing to accept some unusual beliefs: ghost sightings, alien abductions, Jonah Hill's capacity as a filmmaker. A lot of these beliefs are minimally counter-intuitive in the sense that they bear some resemblance to the things we know. For example, ghosts might be disembodied, but there are aspects of them we understand – such as being a conscious person with unfinished business.

Anthropologists think that early gods (with a small 'g') were like this. They inhabited local places and dealt with local hopes and fears. But when human groups grew larger and cities formed, people could no longer know everyone they met, so trust became a problem – it's so much easier to cheat or steal if you think no one knows you. Enter the big, punishing Gods with a capital 'G'.[4] The idea of an all-powerful, all-seeing, vengeful, invisible agent that sees and judges everything you do, took the place of mutual trust between people who knew each other.

Scientists studying the cultural evolution of religions argue that a society in which everyone believed in the same God, enacted rituals together and feared punishment for disobeying the rules would have fewer cheats, and be more harmonious and stable, than other societies.[5] God, whether real or imagined, would have had survival value. They tend to agree with the way the biologist Edward O. Wilson famously put it, 'The genes will always keep culture on a leash', meaning that ideas and behaviours that are biologically adaptive will thrive, while maladaptive ones are weeded out by natural selection.[6]

> Edward O. Wilson (1929–2021) was an immensely influential biologist. As a pioneer of sociobiology, he sought to explain social behaviours through evolutionary theory.

This collaboration between genes and memes makes sense when transmission is largely vertical: when memes are passed down from parent to child. But in the modern world transmission is mostly horizontal: we get our habits and ideas from peers, teachers, internet and media, not just from our parents. In conventional cultural evolution theory, genes retain ultimate control; when we take the memes' eye view we realize that selfish memes may sometimes proliferate entirely for their own sake, not for us, our genes or our societies.

A second replicator

Any evolving system needs information that is copied, varied and selected, meaning that some variants are selected for repeated copying while most disappear. The information is called the 'replicator' and in biology the replicators are genes.[7] This is the creative process that has produced the living world. To make the point that this process is not unique to genes, Richard Dawkins suggested that all the habits, skills, stories, songs and technologies that we copy from person to person are a second replicator evolving on top of the first, and he called them 'memes'.[8] Memes compete for space in our brains and cultures, and we are the human meme machines that copy, vary and select them.[9]

> As organisms, we are 'vehicles' for other entities. These other entities – such as genes or memes – are 'passengers' catching a ride within us. It is the goal of these entities to survive in any way they can. The best means of survival is replication; that's why we call a gene (or a meme) a 'replicator'.

Like genes, memes are selfish information, getting copied whenever and wherever they can, without regard for the consequences. While we constantly try to pick the memes we think are good, true, beautiful or in some way good for us, the memes don't care (because they can't care). They spread for their own benefit, not ours. If a false idea, like an omniscient and punishing God, has what it takes to find a haven in your brain and your life, it will – and it may not be easy to throw it out again.

> According to Blackmore, the idea of God promotes inequality, sexual violence and fear of eternal torment. This is one of the many reasons, she says, for why any description of God as 'all-loving' is a false idea.

So, what does it take? The idea of God is rarely passed on alone but forms part of a co-adapted meme complex, or memeplex. Memeplexes form whenever memes can survive and replicate better together than they could alone. What chance would the idea of the Holy Trinity have on its own? How likely is it that millions of people would simultaneously kneel with their heads on the floor and their bums in the air, five times a day, if this ritual were not part of a package that includes a threatening God who demands they do so on pain of punishment in the afterlife? These memes, these practices, beliefs and ideas, club together into a variety of memeplexes, jostling and competing for survival and replication.

After many centuries of competition, those memes that best exploited human biases, preferences and weaknesses survived to become the ones we face today. In case that seems to imply that memes are little intelligent entities with their own devious plans or intentions, I'll rephrase it: over the centuries, religious memes that happened to exploit human biases, preferences and weaknesses were more likely to be remembered and passed on than those that did not.

And we are rather easy to exploit. We didn't ask to be born, yet here we are, in an often-scary world, with endless decisions to be made, wanting to get things right but not always knowing what is right, longing for love and happiness, fearing pain, fearing the unknown, having strange experiences we don't understand and having no idea what the point of it all is. We long for explanations, comfort, someone who loves us and perhaps for someone to wield justice in an unfair world. Religious memes exploit all of this, not for our benefit, but for their own. The three great monotheistic faiths – Judaism, Christianity and Islam – have gradually beaten countless other competing religions along the way, being honed by memetic selection to fit ever better into our minds and cultures, without caring what harm they do.

These great religions still cling to the biological basis they emerged from: controlling women's bodies to create more babies, promoting 'family values', prohibiting sex before marriage, adultery, homosexuality, masturbation and anything else that would 'waste' semen. God is very good at controlling people's sex lives.

God, men and sex

Judaism, Christianity and Islam have all given power to men, controlled women's fertility and made sure their memes are passed down the generations. Under huge pressure to change, some are slowly changing, arguably becoming more moral and less violent over time.[10] Even so, the most orthodox religious groups still have ferocious rules and spectacularly high fertility rates. Orthodox Jews average roughly seven births per woman, while other Jewish women have only two to three children. Conservative Christians in the United States have more children than liberals; while Christians have between 1.9 and 2.5 births, non-believers are well below, with atheists at 1.6 and agnostics at only 1.3 births per woman.[11, 12]

Orthodox versions of the big three still maintain strict rules that keep women making babies – babies fathered only by the men who control them. This is a form of 'mate guarding', as seen in many birds, mammals and amphibians. For sexual species like us, the male produces lots of sperm, so one strategy for passing on his genes is to have as much sex as possible, never mind the childcare. Even if he does his share of caring, it is still (genetically) worthwhile to find sex elsewhere if he can. Females, meanwhile, can have only a few children in their lifetime and need to be choosy about their mates, whether they choose one who will provide good child support or one with good genes that will produce sexy sons (or possibly both).[13] Unlike women, men cannot know for sure whether a baby is their own, so they risk being cuckolded – putting time, effort and resources into bringing up another man's child – unless they guard their women. Islam, in particular, gives clear instructions on how women are to be controlled.[14]

By contrast, today's secular memes are rapidly breaking away from biological sex differences, yet we can still see mate guarding in those creepy men who try to control their partners' lives, from what she wears and how she looks to where she goes and whom she meets. In the modern world we call this 'coercive control', and in some countries this is now a criminal offence. Yet for an Orthodox Jew or observant Muslim, coercive control is not just allowed, it is obligatory.

In Muslim Saudi Arabia young girls and boys are segregated, girls must be completely covered in public so that no unrelated man can see their skin (apart from a little around their eyes), marriages are arranged and married women must stay in their homes unless permitted, and escorted, by a male guardian who may even be one of their young sons. Some women can never leave the house at all.

Absher© is a smartphone application produced by the Saudi Arabian government. The app, which boasts tens of millions of users, allows 'guardians' (*Wali*) to track the locations of women. A rough translation of 'Absher' is 'Yes, Sir.'

There's even an app called 'Absher' to help men control 'their' women.

In Orthodox Judaism, a woman may first meet her husband-to-be on the day of the wedding. Once married, she must follow a strict timetable for sex that is clearly designed to coincide with ovulation. After a period, she checks with a white cloth that the bleeding has stopped, sometimes needing a Rabbi to check. Seven days after the cloth is clean, she has a *mikvah,* or ritual bath, to ensure she is clean enough to have sex with her husband, whether she wants it or not.

Meanwhile, something very interesting is happening. The rest of culture has broken away from biology. As travel and communications get faster and more efficient, memes spread further and faster around the world. Science, literature and technology provide countless new ideas that compete with religion for space in people's lives and cultures, and genes are too slow to keep up. This makes a big difference to religions that began, evolved and grew powerful by serving their followers' genetic success but now find themselves in a world of high-speed communications in which genetic advantage is barely relevant. We have birth control and may choose to have few children or none. With radio, television, phones, cars, trains, planes, the internet and social media, we spread ideas of sexual and racial equality, freedom of speech, freedom of belief, equality before the law and the rights of the child. We prioritize human flourishing and happiness over biological reproduction: we choose human rights over genes.

The God meme hates human rights.

The structure of a memeplex

Religions, like other vast memeplexes, resemble organisms. They have internal structures, boundaries, that protect and keep them together and numerous constituent memes all of which need tricks of some kind to earn, and keep, their place in the whole. By calling these 'tricks', I don't mean that a magician invented them to trick people, rather that with all the variety of ideas and practices that came up over the centuries, the ones that did trick people into adopting them survived the longest.

The most wicked trick of all is the God meme's great weapon – His threats and promises. Give us heaven and hell, give us some really horrifying threats and deliciously tempting promises, with a judging God who decides who gets which, and we may be too scared to disobey. Of course, we might be tempted to doubt the existence of these realms, but part of the trick is that heaven and hell are invisible until we die. This trick looks so childish that it's hard to believe that people go on believing it, but they do. It works because we have a natural tendency towards dualism, to thinking that our minds are separate from our bodies and because it preys on our deepest hopes and fears.

We all fear pain and can imagine horrible ways of its being inflicted. So, it's not surprising that the Christian and Islamic hells are full of fires that burn forever and hideous creatures that enjoy tormenting the damned. Each chapter of the Holy Qur'an begins with the words, 'In the Name of Allāh, the Compassionate, the Merciful.' Yet this 'compassionate' God decrees that 'Garments of fire have been prepared for the unbelievers. Scalding water shall be poured upon their heads, melting their skins and that which is in their bellies. They shall be lashed with rods of iron.' And, if they try to escape, angels will drag them back to taste the 'torments of hell-fire'.[15]

Somali-born author Ayaan Hirsi Ali describes a Muslim childhood in Africa blighted by violence and threats of hell.[16] If she made a mistake in reciting the Qur'an or failed to obey all the taboos and restrictions that apply to girls, she would be threatened with a hell of 'sores, boiling water, peeling skin, burning flesh, dissolving bowels, the everlasting fire that burns you forever, for as your flesh chars and your juices boil, you form a new skin. . . . The thirst causes so much pain that

As a Muslim, Ayaan Hirsi Ali was the victim of beatings, genital mutilation and forced marriage. After she denounced Islam, she became the target of death threats and her friend, Theo van Gogh, was murdered. Today, she is one of Islam's most influential critics.

you start wailing for water whereupon the juices from your burning body are thrown into your mouth.'[17] What child ever deserves to be threatened this way?

Heaven is much harder to imagine than hell, especially for modern people living fast-moving and fulfilling lives. Sitting next to Jesus with angels playing harps on clouds is laughable, and there is little appeal to the cooling streams, delicious fruits and dazzling jewels that Allāh has prepared for the faithful. But perhaps the seventy-two houri, or virgins, said to await the martyr would appeal to some in this rather obvious fourteenth-century male fantasy. Could we try to imagine more tempting modern heavens? Would enhanced senses, greater intelligence and infinite broadband streamed straight into our heavenly heads do the trick? I'm certainly not tempted by one modern male fantasy, the heaven of the Church of the Flying Spaghetti Monster with its beer volcano and stripper factory. It seems we have a concept of 'eternal joy and happiness' but little idea what that means.

> The Church of the Flying Spaghetti Monster is a satirical religion. Controversially, 'Pastafarian' hell also includes beer and strippers; however, the beer is flat, and its inhabitants suffer from STIs.

Other meme tricks help support the whole construction. In case you begin to argue or express doubts about your religion, there's the idea that faith is intrinsically 'good', regardless of how you behave. Doubts about God must occur to almost everyone at some time, so the faith trick helps to keep even the most curious and sceptical followers in line if they are infected with the meme that faith is good, and doubt is bad.

> According to Judaism, Christianity and Islam, faith is an intrinsic good. This virtue is illustrated, by each tradition, through the story of Abraham's (attempted) sacrifice of his son. God tells Abraham to kill his son Isaac; when he agrees, God gets cold feet and asks him to stop. Abraham is praised for his obedience.

Even beauty can help attract and retain followers. Wonderful music and art, glorious buildings, beautiful sculptures and sacred objects can bring people to religion and keep them there. The beauty of a great mosque or synagogue might encourage them to join in rituals of prayer and devotion. They may visit a fabulous cathedral to enjoy the singing, candles and company, but find themselves gazing at images of crucifixion and martyred saints or being reminded of their own sinful wickedness and urged to follow Jesus for redemption.

Altruism and our natural desire to be good (or at least, to appear good) become meme tricks when 'good' is redefined to mean what helps the memes rather than what helps the people who spread them. Worshipping God makes you a 'good' person; believing in Him makes you 'good'; obeying His random rules and rituals makes you 'good'. Giving money to your church makes you 'good' even if (indeed because) your money is used to spread more of God's memes. Passing on your faith to your children is 'good', as is forcing your faith on someone you marry and insisting, as the Catholic Church does, that children must be brought up in the faith. 'Spread the good news' of Jesus is the simplest kind of meme trick, containing a 'copy me' instruction as in a chain letter or email virus.

Truth itself turns to trickery when religions claim that theirs is 'the *one* truth', 'the *only* truth' and that everything you'll ever need to know is written in their one oh-so-Holy book. But for the truth trick to work, people must be kept away from alternative books and ideas and from the meme-spreading technologies that can undermine that 'Truth'. In Afghanistan, the Taliban are doing this ferociously – preventing girls from going to school, and outlawing music, television and even reading. Boys can go to school, but mostly learn to recite the Qur'an and the rules of Islam rather than learning about the outside world.

Curiosity and new ideas pose the greatest threat to the God meme. When Ayaan Hirsi Ali eventually escaped to the Netherlands and began studying at university, almost everything she read challenged her as a Muslim. 'Drinking wine and wearing trousers were nothing compared to reading the history of ideas', she wrote.[18] She finally rejected her faith, but despite all she had gone through, it was still hard to do. And Islam has one more protective strategy for itself: kill the infidel.[19] Ayaan, therefore, lives with frequent threats of death and under the constant protection of bodyguards.

> The term 'infidel' is derogatory; it is used to describe a person who rejects the doctrines of another person's faith. Hirsi Ali points out that her persecution was instructed by the Qur'an; 'Women were worth half a man. Infidels should be killed.'

I have painted a picture of selfish memeplexes that exploit human beings for their own benefit. An example comes from extensive research into the medieval witch persecutions during which an estimated forty to fifty thousand 'witches' were executed.[20] Beliefs about flying witches, nightly sabbats with the Devil and cruel methods for trying to get rid of them, formed a memeplex that spread effectively even though no one appears to have gained anything.

Individuals were harmed along with their genes, families were broken up, trust destroyed and whole communities were devastated. Only the memes benefitted.

God's kingdoms

Have I missed something important? All these God religions promote kindness, love, generosity and caring for others. Shouldn't we expect these qualities to flourish in believers? Some believers undoubtedly find happiness, and some a lifetime's spiritual path leading to love, compassion, insight and equanimity. Perhaps they ignore the worst of what their faith teaches and are inspired instead by stories of Jesus welcoming prostitutes and lepers, overthrowing the moneychangers' tables, praising 'faith, hope and charity', or his final words, 'Father, forgive them, for they know not what they do.' If these effects were the norm, we might expect people in religious countries to behave especially well, and religious societies to be happier, healthier and less dysfunctional than secular or non-religious ones. Are they?

No. The opposite is true. This disturbing correlation was found by researcher Gregory Paul, who compared religiosity in the prosperous democracies with scores on the 'Successful Societies Scale'.[21] This includes rates of homicide, suicide, teenage pregnancy, sexually transmitted disease, marital breakdown, levels of incarceration and abortion – precisely the kinds of societal ills that religions so often rail against. He found that higher rates of belief in and worship of a creator correlated with higher, not lower, rates of homicide, juvenile and early adult mortality, STD infection rates, teenage pregnancy and abortion. I find the differences in rates of abortion particularly upsetting, because in the United States, where the religious right is fighting to make abortion illegal and getting one can be difficult and expensive, there are actually more abortions than there are in the United Kingdom where women can choose, and abortions are free on request.

All this seems tragic and unnecessary to me. We now know that societies can function perfectly well without God's coercion even if it was useful in the past. Indeed, it is generally the most religious societies that are the poorest, least healthy and least happy. When a Gallup survey asked people in 114 countries how important religion is to their lives, they found that in the world's poorest countries (average per capita income of $2,000 or less) the median proportion who said religion was important to them was ninety-five per cent, while in the richest countries (where the average income was above $25,000) it was only forty-seven per cent.[22] Other studies confirm a strong negative correlation between religiosity and GDP. *The World Happiness Report*, published by the United Nations, ranks countries based on respondents' ratings of their own lives.[23] In 2022, a familiar list of countries made the top five for happiness – Finland, Denmark, Iceland, Switzerland and The Netherlands – all low in religious observance. The bottom five were Botswana, Rwanda, Zimbabwe, Lebanon and Afghanistan, countries with many religions and few people who claim to have no religion. The United States and the United Kingdom come sixteenth and seventeenth.[24] Although these correlations may tempt us to infer that religion causes poverty and unhappiness, further research suggests that the poor and desperate turn to religion for comfort and support. This may explain why the wealthy, and moderately happy, United States is so religious: it has no well-functioning welfare state or healthcare system. Perhaps religion is a sticking plaster for fear, distress, sickness and poverty, one that can safely be discarded only when real solutions are found.

Those who believe in God, who follow a religion that relies on God, are being cheated. These are just some of the reasons why I say that God is one of the nastiest and most powerful memes that has ever evolved.

Afterthoughts

Blackmore's argument isn't just that believing in God is irrational, but that it's dangerous. Religions are memeplexes that conceal their true natures with ideas of goodness and generosity; however, lurking behind their veils are notions that serve only to benefit the memes and, at our expense, perpetuate an intolerance for moral progress. Following Blackmore, it's important to keep in mind that the natural sciences are memeplexes too; yet there's a big difference between God memes and science memes. Science is constantly testing itself, but religion refuses to be tested. It's no wonder that for anybody who doesn't fulfil God's conservative, eternal will – or the will of the heterosexual male – religion can be a miserable affair.

At the same time, it's important to recognize that religion can be a force for a lot of good. There are many of people who claim their lives are deeply enriched by God. When they're suffering, when they're lonely, when nothing else can help them: belief that someone is watching over them and that things will work out in the end is their only light in the darkness. In this sense, the God meme isn't just exploiting us – it's giving us hope. No doubt, however, the Church has a long and shameful history of persecuting

those who oppose the God meme – guilting, shaming, inquisiting, crusading – but the vices of control and violence aren't unique to religion. Mao's China, Hitler's Germany, Stalin's Soviet Union: when it comes to terrible memeplexes, we're not short of examples. Perhaps the God meme in its *purest* aspect – as nothing more than an explanatory hypothesis – looks a little different to the God of organized religion; however, even this, says our next contributor, is a barrier to scientific progress.

Questions to consider

1. How does the God meme differ from the science meme?
2. Can an explanation of theism's origin undermine the legitimacy of religious belief?
3. Are some religions less dangerous than others?
4. Why do you think the God meme is so powerful?
5. Does the God meme hate human rights?

Recommended reading

Advanced

Susan Blackmore, *The Meme Machine* (Oxford: Oxford University Press, 1999).

> A landmark text in the field, this is the best introduction to memes that's out there. The book discusses the nature of memes – the chapters on sex and religion are excellent – and several problems facing memetics. This is important reading for those interested in questions of cultural evolution and personal identity.

The Oxford Handbook of Atheism, ed. Stephen Bullivant and Michael Ruse (Oxford: Oxford University Press, 2013).

> This is a collection of short papers discussing the atheist worldview. The book covers the nature of atheism, its history, atheist philosophies – Humanism, Buddhism, Hinduism and so forth – as well as atheism's relationship with science and art.

Intermediate

Ayaan Hirsi Ali, *Infidel: My Life* (London: Simon & Schuster, 2007).

> Ayaan Hirsi Ali is a social and political activist, and one of Islam's most formidable opponents. This is her autobiography; the book's key themes

are Islam's subjection of women, hostility towards moral progress and divinely sanctioned extremism.

Robert Wright, *The Evolution of God: The Origins of Our Beliefs* (London: Little, Brown, 2009).

The topic here isn't philosophy of religion, but the history of religion. Wright approaches the subject from the perspective of evolutionary psychology, taking his reader from the beliefs of early tribes to the God of the Abrahamic monotheisms.

Beginner

Susan Blackmore, 'Why I Have Given Up', *Skeptical Odysseys: Personal Accounts by the World's Leading Paranormal Inquirers*, ed. Paul Kurtz (Amherst, NY: Prometheus Books, 2001): 85–94.

An insightful, short reflection on why Blackmore – after twenty-five years of research in parapsychology – abandoned her belief in the paranormal. This article contains a lot of great examples from Blackmore's research, illustrating the pull of the paranormal and her reasons for embracing scepticism.

Christopher Hitchens, *God Is Not Great: The Case Against Religion* (London: Atlantic Books, 2007).

Like Blackmore's chapter, the spirit of Hitchens's book is one of anti-theism – the belief that religion causes more evil than good. Hitchens argues that religion is a human invention that restricts our scientific understanding and inflicts a great deal of suffering on the world's people. As Hitchens puts it, 'religion poisons everything'.[25]

Chapter Six

Why I'm an Atheist

Richard Dawkins

Introduction

Charles Darwin's *On the Origin of Species* is a strong contender for the most important text in the history of human thought.[1] Just take a moment to reflect on the complexity of the natural world: the flight of a hummingbird, the sprint of a cheetah, the breath of a whale, a daisy turning towards the sunlight. Before Darwin, the argument from design was one of the best arguments for God. Today, however, we know exactly how and why the world's creatures, ourselves included, exhibit such physical complexity. God didn't create us over a weekend: every single living thing is here because its genes were passed down, generation to generation, through the long and arduous process of <u>natural selection</u>.

In this chapter, we'll be discussing evolution and atheism with Professor Richard Dawkins. It's no exaggeration to say that Richard is the world's most famous atheist. His contributions to evolutionary biology have been revolutionary and his books – including *The Selfish Gene*,[2] *The Blind Watchmaker*,[3] and *The God Delusion*[4] – have a readership in the tens of millions. In the light of his influence, it's no wonder that Dawkins has been named *the* world's top thinker.[5]

Charles Darwin (1809–1882) discovered that variations within an organism's genetic code may increase its chances of survival and, therefore, the likelihood of it reproducing. Given enough time, this process removes ill-adapted lifeforms while preserving those which have adjusted to their environment. This is 'evolution by <u>natural selection</u>'.

For Dawkins, believing in God is like believing in Santa Claus, Superman or a decent Adam Sandler movie. We can't guarantee their non-existence, but we can be very, very confident that they don't exist. Dawkins accepts there are mysteries to be solved – consciousness, for example, and the laws and origin of the universe – but he sees no point in bringing God into these discussions. When we place our faith in God, we betray the spirit of Darwin and the quest for genuine answers. God, says Dawkins, is a pernicious delusion that ought to go extinct.

Darwin's heir

Before we discuss the philosophy of religion, I wonder what you think about the nature of philosophy more generally. Do you think that philosophy can help us understand the world?

I see philosophy as the study of how we think and what we mean by certain words. These are important things to consider; however, I'm never quite sure why scientists can't figure these things out for themselves. (In fact, they often do.) I suppose philosophers have the advantage of a long history of thought, from Plato onwards, so they know what kind of mistakes we've made in the past. Therefore, they probably have something useful to contribute. In particular, I admire the philosophical technique of the *gedankenexperiment* – I find it to be a valuable trick for thinking. In some ways, the role of philosophy is to *help* scientists formulate questions and ideas. With that said, philosophy isn't going to make much progress on its own. For progress, we need science.

> The German word for 'thought experiment' is *'gedankenexperiment'*.

How did you become interested in questions of philosophy and science – questions of God, evolution and the origin of life?

I've always been a bookish kind of person, and, as a boy, I was interested in the deep, philosophical questions of existence. I drifted into biology because of those questions – my father's education in science was another inspiration. By the time I arrived at university, I was immersed in Darwin's world. What fascinated me about Darwinian evolution was that it answered, as far as biology is concerned, the most profound question of all: how we came to have a planet with such beautifully complicated things which look – to the untrained eye – as if they were designed. Darwin had, to my mind, knocked the stuffing out of theism.

Was it your exposure to Darwin that changed your thinking about God, or have you always considered yourself an atheist?

Like most children, I was raised in an educational environment that was theistic, so I used to believe in God. Many children find themselves brainwashed by priests, parents and teachers who force them to believe in eternal hellfire and that women are the property of men. I was lucky enough to be exposed to other ideas; I owe it to my parents that they taught me *how* to think and not *what* to think. I remember reading Bertrand Russell in the school library – 'Why I am Not a Christian',[6] 'What I Believe'[7] – but the power of Darwinian evolution finally broke it for me.

> The philosopher Bertrand Russell (1872–1970) was a strong opponent of religious belief. In 'Why I am not a Christian', he tells us that the basis of religion is fear – 'fear of the mysterious, fear of defeat and fear of death'.

Atheism's a broad church, representing people from a wealth of different backgrounds. What do you think it means to be an atheist?

Different people mean different things by 'atheism'. On the one hand, some say that atheism is the *positive* belief that there's nothing supernatural; on the other, some define it as a *lack* of belief in the supernatural. In my book, *The God Delusion*, I formulated a seven-point scale from 'belief' to 'disbelief'.[8] A 'one' on the scale claims to *know* that there *is* a God. (Carl Jung is a good example of this.)[9] At the other end, a 'seven' claims to *know* there *isn't* a God. I'd put myself at a 6.9. Though, the remaining 0.1 isn't anything to get carried away by: it's not really saying much. I'd say the same thing about leprechauns or fairies; I can't be *sure* there aren't leprechauns in hidden underground caves or fairies at the bottom of my garden. Strictly speaking, we should all be agnostics about leprechauns but, if pressed, we'd accept that they didn't exist; the same is true for God. Agnosticism implies a fifty-fifty chance of God existing, which is very different to my view. That's why I describe myself as an 'atheist'.

> In a televised interview, the analytic psychologist Carl Jung (1875–1961) was asked whether he believed in God. Jung replied, 'I *know*. I don't need to believe. I know.'

Are there any beliefs that you'd give a 'seven' on your scale? Something that has *absolutely* no chance of existing?

I suppose I'd give a 'seven' to formal contradictions, like square-circles and married-bachelors. God's very close though . . . it's probably a bit cowardly to say He's a '6.9'. Let's call it '6.999'.

The blind watchmaker

People are, quite understandably, blown away by the natural world's complexity. In the nineteenth century, the philosopher William Paley tapped into this sense of admiration and argued that the world's fine-tuned mechanisms – such as the human eye or a bee's sting – resemble machines like telescopes and pocket watches.[10] What would you say to those who believe that nature is evidence of intelligent design?

> The most famous version of the argument from design was devised by William Paley (1743–1805). The opening passages of his book *Natural Theology* (1802), where he compares the complexity of a watch with that of nature, are considered mandatory reading for all students of philosophy.

If you believe that nature is evidence of intelligent design, then you haven't understood the literature. The eye is an excellent example of this and one that Darwin discussed himself. Darwin said that the eye worried him: he thought its ability to detect light and focus on different distances was astounding.[11] Creationists like to pretend that this is an example of irreducible complexity. However, Darwin was just luring his opponents in for the kill. The eye didn't worry him at all; he had a perfectly good explanation for it. The steps by which the eye evolved can be easily understood in terms of physics and biology.

> Some proponents of intelligent design claim that biological systems exhibit features of irreducible complexity: natural phenomena that cannot be explained as the result of a chain of modifications of previously functioning organisms.

The eye, said Darwin, evolved over hundreds of millions of years in slow, gradual degrees. Looking around the animal kingdom, you find all of the intermediate stages: half-eyes, quarter-eyes, eighth-eyes, tenth-eyes and three-quarter-eyes. They're all there; there's no irreducible complexity. It's easy to think of cases when an eighth of an eye will be better than a tenth of an eye; for one, it will give you a slightly better chance of spotting predators. The final perfection of an eye, in something like an eagle, is just the end product of a whole series of gradual, incremental stages and improvements. Still, even if that weren't the case – even if biologists were so baffled by a particular phenomenon that they accepted they didn't know how it evolved – that still wouldn't be evidence of intelligent design. There's no need to fill the gaps with God.

To take another example of irreducible complexity, one might think that the intermediary stages between having 'no wing' and a 'full wing' won't increase your chances of survival. What good is half a wing? If you can't fly, don't wings just slow you down?

That's an interesting question with an equally interesting answer. You have a *slightly* greater chance of being airborne with half a wing, a quarter-wing or a tenth-wing than you do with no wing. For example, suppose you're a squirrel leaping from one branch to another. Without any wing, you can jump a certain distance – let's say one metre. However, if you have a *slight* increase in surface area – a small membrane stretched between your arms and ribs – you'll increase

the distance you can leap without falling to the ground. If you can leap a metre without that little membrane, you might reach an extra half a metre with an increased surface area. In the forest, over millions of years, that's the difference between extinction and survival. Today, in the forests of Africa, Australia and South-East Asia, you can see animals with membranes that stretch from their arms to their legs. They can't exactly fly, but they can glide quite gracefully and use this to land safely on lower branches. While they're gliding, they manipulate their

The <u>flying squirrel</u>

limbs and steer themselves around. That's not all that different from flapping; it's not a massive leap from '<u>flying squirrel</u>' to bat. What's the use of half a wing? If you understand biology, it's not really a problem.

There are a lot of philosophers who think that minor, incremental changes will never be able to explain the existence of (seemingly non-physical) consciousness. Do you see consciousness as a threat to evolutionary biology?

Consciousness is the biggest mystery facing science. We don't know at what stage it arose, and it's not even clear what consciousness does for you which couldn't be done by a non-conscious robot. You could program a robot to do most of the things that humans do and fool somebody into thinking the robot was conscious. I don't know whether fish are conscious, and I don't know whether newts are conscious, yet I'd be pretty surprised if chimpanzees and dogs weren't. Consciousness manifests itself in physical brains when they reach a certain level of complexity. That means something about the evolution of the brain leads to consciousness, so no, it's not a threat. Sure, it's a mystery, but it's not a mystery to be solved by introducing supernatural souls. That's just a cop-out.

Suppose you were born *before* Darwin published *On the Origin of Species*. If you read Paley's work in 1802, for example, do you think you would have been more inclined to accept the argument from design?

I would have been, yes. Darwin himself read *Natural Theology* in college and was very persuaded by it. I suppose I would have been too. I used to say that before Darwin, it would have been very difficult to be an atheist.[12] I no longer think that's true; theism has never been a coherent worldview. If I were alive in 1802, I would have accepted that I don't understand nature's complexity, but that – whatever the explanation is – theism is not the answer. 'There must be something else', I'd say. 'Let's get to work and see what it is.'

Twiddling the knobs of creation

Rather than appealing to nature, religious philosophers are beginning to appeal to the laws of physics as evidence for design. For example, Richard Swinburne has argued that God is the simplest explanation for the universe's finely tuned <u>constants</u>. Is this a better argument for intelligent design?

Certainly not in the way that Swinburne puts it. Theists portray God as some kind of Divine Knob-Twiddler: when God decided to set up the universe, He tuned all of the fundamental constants to create galaxies, stars and life. If that sounds farfetched, consider what God must *be* in order to twiddle the knobs of creation: He would have to be *as complex* and improbable as the universe's laws. Swinburne's argument just kicks the can down the road.

Now, there are some genuine attempts at explaining the laws of the universe. For example, a popular theory among physicists

> Specific laws of physics are required for the existence of stars and planets. If these <u>constants</u> weren't constant, the universe would be inhospitable to life. For example, if the cosmological constant (the rate of the universe's expansion) had been slightly higher, gravity couldn't have formed stars and planets; yet, if it had been smaller, the universe would have collapsed in on itself.

is the multiverse hypothesis. One of the consequences of the <u>inflationary model</u> of the universe is that you have a vast number of universes existing in parallel. Each of these universes has different values of the fundamental constants, and we occupy one of the universes in which the constants produce galaxies, planets, chemistry and life. If the multiverse theory is correct, then we can account for fine-tuning. I should emphasize, however, that even if the multiverse theory is false, then the God-theory wouldn't be any better off. Theism just says, 'God did it! Sorry, we're not taking any questions at the moment.' It just lies down and gives up. In the light of Darwin, we should all be suspicious of theists who tell us that the world is the product of miraculous design. In contrast, science goes on working, asking questions and trying to unravel the mysteries of nature.

> According to the <u>inflationary model</u>, the earliest moments of our universe involved a period of exponential growth, after which our universe expanded at a much slower rate. Some physicists maintain that inflation is *eternal* and, therefore, leads to multiple exponential expansions; these expansions slow down to form multiple universes.

Would you give a similar response to the cosmological argument? If the universe had a beginning, and everything that begins to exist has a cause, does that mean the universe has a cause?

The universe may have a cause, and whatever produced the Big Bang will have to be very simple. So, that rules out God. What we need is a proper explanation. As an evolutionary biologist, I'm accustomed to the Darwinian idea of something relatively simple developing into complexity. We need something like that in cosmology.

Do you have any thoughts on what that 'something' might be?

You'd have to ask a physicist. In <u>Lawrence Krauss</u>'s book, *A Universe from Nothing*, he answers in terms of quantum theory.[13] I can repeat his words, but that doesn't mean I understand them. What I can say, however, is this: what biologists did for life, we need physicists to do for the rest of the universe. We spoke about Paley earlier. Paley thought that *life* – not the universe – was by far the best argument for God. He rather skated over the world's existence; he mentions Saturn's

> <u>Lawrence Krauss</u> is a popular theoretical physicist. In his book, *A Universe from Nothing: Why There Is Something Rather than Nothing* (2012), Krauss explains how the universe evolved from fundamental laws of nature. As to the origin of these laws, Krauss describes them as 'random' values that could have been 'almost everything' and, therefore, 'no entity' is required to fix them.

ring as the only complex, non-biological thing in the universe.[14] The universe didn't give him much pause; he went straight to biology. Darwin solved the mystery of life and that should give physicists a great deal of courage.

In your book, *The Selfish Gene*, you describe nature as 'red in tooth and claw'. However, for many religious believers, nature is precisely the opposite. For example, Paley tells us that the 'air, the earth and the water, teem with delighted existence'. 'A bee amongst the flowers', he says, 'is one of the cheerfullest objects that could be looked upon. Its life appears to be all enjoyment: so busy, and so pleased.'[15] Is happiness not the rule and misery the exception?

> The phrase, 'red in tooth and claw' refers to the remorseless bloodshed of nature. The line was first used by Alfred Tennyson (1809–1892) in his poem, *In Memoriam A. H. H.* (1850).

You can pick your examples to illustrate the benevolence of nature; however, you can do the opposite just as well. Darwin pointed towards the Ichneumonidae, a group of parasitic wasps that lay their eggs in the caterpillars of other insects; the larvae hatch out and eat their victims alive from within.[16] Darwin held up this example and said, approximately, 'I can't believe that a benevolent deity would create something so awful.' Of course, millions of animals die suffering – from parasites, predators and starvation. If you look at lions, they're designed to kill antelopes; look at antelopes and they're designed to run from lions. You have to ask whose side God's on. If you're cherry-picking your examples, you can make whatever case you like.

> The Ichneumonidae (also known as 'Darwin wasps') have been studied since the time of Aristotle (384–322 BCE), who coined their name in his book, *The History of Animals* (c. 350 BCE). Reflecting on the wasp, Darwin writes, 'I own that I cannot see as plainly as others do, and as I should wish to do, evidence of design and beneficence on all sides of us. There seems to me too much misery in the world.'

Happiness is not the rule. Yet, that doesn't mean that selfish misery is the rule either. It's unfortunate that the title of my book, *The Selfish Gene*, is taken to mean that animals are selfish. It doesn't mean that; it means that *genes* are selfish. Genes look after their own interests and do whatever they can to survive through the generations. If that means making individual animals selfish, so be it. However, genes can also benefit from altruistic animals. That's why nature can be both selfish and altruistic. There are lots of animals who will save each other from predators, for example, even if it puts them at serious risk. That's their genes at work.

Do you think these examples of natural suffering are a problem for theists who believe in an all-loving God?

There are philosophers who say that the problem of evil is 'the most powerful objection' to theism. I don't think that's right. If I were a theologian, I would say, 'Well, maybe God's just evil.' After all, this is only an argument against a *good* God. Goodness is just an add-on; there are loads of gods to which evil is irrelevant. The point, however, is that no version of God can withstand scientific scrutiny and, therefore, there are powerful reasons for rejecting the gods of every religion.

The good life

Some academics like to cite your philosophy as an example of <u>moral subjectivism</u>. 'Here's Richard Dawkins,' they say, 'arguing that morality is only there to ensure our survival.' On atheism, is morality anything more than a survival mechanism?

I don't fall back on Darwinism for morality. I think that morality arises by intelligent design. (Don't take that out of context.) We have moral philosophy – virtue ethics, Kantian ethics, utilitarian ethics – and all sorts of arguments that are born out of human culture. The history of ethics is a long philosophical, jurisprudential, parliamentary, journalistic, civilized discussion. The moral

> Moral objectivism claims that morality is mind-*independent*. In contrast, moral subjectivism states that morality is mind-*dependent* – on this view, our moral principles are grounded in culture, evolution and individual preferences.

standards of any particular time are very different from those of earlier centuries. It seems, by our standards, that things are getting better: we no longer believe in slavery, we no longer send little boys up chimneys, women have more rights and animals have better protections. Those are all sorts of ways in which the twenty-first century's standards are different to those of our ancestors. If you sat down to read something even as recent as <u>Agatha Christie</u>, for example, you would find all kinds of sexist, racist language that have no place in modern Europe. Things change according to the shifting moral zeitgeist. This is nothing to do with religion and nothing to do with holy books. There's something, as it were, in the air of the time. If we did base our morality on religion, we'd still be stoning people to death for committing adultery

> <u>Agatha Christie</u> (1890–1976) is *the* bestselling novelist of all time. This is no place for examples of Christie's inflammatory language – including the original title of her book, *And Then There Were None* (1939).

and breaking the Sabbath. From a moral point of view, the Bible is hideous.

It's interesting that you describe the history of ethics as changing for the 'better'. If morality is grounded in particular societies, how can we judge the societies of the past?

Well, what we're doing is measuring the ethics of past societies against our own standards. It's possible that Henry VIII would disagree with our way of thinking, but I can still judge his views to be worse or better than mine. Now, one thing I would say to Henry VIII is that he shouldn't get his morality from the Bible. In fact, like most people today, he rarely did so. Americans love to talk about the Ten Commandments; most of them don't even know what the Ten Commandments are. With a few exceptions, like the Sermon on the Mount, I defy anybody to find anything in the Bible that, by modern standards, is morally sound. It may be a good work of fiction, but the Bible is an awful moral guide.

What if a believer cites historical evidence – Moses's parting of the Red Sea, Christ's resurrection or Muhammad's flight to heaven – to support the legitimacy of their holy text?

There's no decent evidence that any of those things happened. I'm accustomed to people who dig their toes in about Jesus's resurrection. When influential people pass away, like Elvis Presley or Princess Diana, legends start to abound. Jesus was just another charismatic figure whose disciples were desperate to see him again. I mean, at least the legends of Elvis and Diana were written immediately after their deaths – the Gospels were written decades after Jesus's crucifixion. That is, if he even existed.

Echoing Blaise Pascal, Daniel Hill has argued that being an atheist isn't worth the risk. If there is *any* risk of heaven and hell – even a 0.001 chance – then it is irrational to reject belief in God.

If God really cares so desperately about people believing in Him, what a narcissistic, megalomaniac He must be. Why does He care so much about people believing in Him? Is He insecure? Why not reward people for being good instead? I doubt that even Pascal thought much of this argument. Even if he did, why did he think that he'd be rewarded with eternal happiness? Which God was he even talking about? Zeus? Poseidon? Wotan? The idea that God prefers dishonest belief over honest scepticism is baffling. Pascal's Wager is a stupid argument.

> Wotan (also known as 'Odin') was the chief god of the Vikings. Father of Thor, Wotan was a god of war; he rode along the battlefield on an eight-legged steed and sold one of his eyes for wisdom.

You've said in the past that you'd prefer the number of religious believers to fall to zero. What would you say to those who claim that believing in God increases their well-being?

People can get comfort and happiness from all sorts of things, falsehoods included. For example, I can imagine patients who wouldn't want their doctor telling them if they had a terminal illness; they would be happier, they say, if the doctor lied to them. At the same time, some people would prefer their doctor to tell them the truth – I know I certainly would. To my mind, it would be a betrayal of everything that science stands for to abandon reason and believe in the supernatural so I could 'feel better' about my life. In many ways, I regard *The God Delusion* as a scientific book because I consider theism to be a scientific hypothesis. Believing that there is a prime mover or creative intelligence at the base of the universe is to say something about how the world works. I'm a lover of truth, which means scientific truth. I hope to inspire others to feel the same. Remember, it's religion – not science – that inspires suicide bombers and witch-hunts.

Do you think that atheists can have the best of both worlds? Can they reject the supernatural while engaging with religion's spiritual traditions, such as meditation or mindfulness?

I think so, yes. My colleague <u>Sam Harris</u>, for example, says that meditation is a physiological exercise with many benefits. Meditation doesn't have to be religious. Yet, I think we can push this even further. As an atheist, I see no reason why I can't enjoy the sacred music of Bach and Mozart or the world's beautiful cathedrals. Wherever I go, I love to look at cathedrals. I find them deeply moving – they're magnificent, beautiful buildings. Mind you, I don't find ordinary church services that moving; in fact, I find them either

> Sam Harris is a neuroscientist and philosopher. His bestselling book, *The End of Faith: Religion, Terror, and the Future of Reason* (2004), established Harris's name as a leading proponent of atheism. Sam has been meditating for over thirty years; his popular mobile application, *Waking Up*, offers meditative guides from leading practitioners.

boring or, in the happy clappy case, pathetically embarrassing.

Out of all the arguments for God – design, cosmological, ontological, well-being and scripture – are there any that you find more convincing than others?

It's a pretty tough job thinking about which arguments are more convincing than others. I mean, they're all rubbish. I suppose the least convincing are arguments from scripture; you might as well get your beliefs from any other book in the library. I would say that the fine-tuning argument is a little trickier. I don't think it's a very good argument, but I don't know enough physics to demolish it in the same way that a physicist could. The only one you listed that we haven't discussed is the ontological argument; that deserves a special mention for being one of the worst arguments in history. I can't understand why anybody would take it seriously. The idea that you could reach a conclusion about something as grand and important as the universe by sitting in your armchair and logic-chopping . . . well, it's demeaning. For the same reason, that's why I'm hostile to fundamentalist religion: it stays inside, locks its doors and shelters itself from scientific enterprise. Religion teaches us not to change our minds – not to go outside and learn exciting, new things about the world. That's why I'm an atheist: religion saps the intellect.

Afterthoughts

Dawkins's enthusiasm for science is contagious and, in virtue of his honesty and humour, it's easy to see how he has managed to rile up so many theists. Throughout the world, millions of people continue to reject Darwin's insight – and these people don't take kindly to Richard's

no-nonsense rhetoric. The spirit of this hostility is illustrated by the right-wing commentator Ann Coulter, who defies any of her co-religionists to tell her 'they do not laugh at the idea of Dawkins burning in hell'.[17] He clearly touches a nerve. Philosophically, however, there's no competition. Even the philosophers of our opening chapters – some of the world's most significant philosophers of religion – don't even mention the argument from biology. Paley's argument is of the past, not the future.

These days, religious philosophers tend to favour the argument from fine-tuning. As you'll remember, Swinburne's case for theism rested on the idea that God is a 'simple' hypothesis. Dawkins offered an interesting response: he told us that God, if She's going to dispose every atom in the universe – let alone create life, consciousness and listen to everybody's prayers – isn't going to be a simple entity but an incredibly complex one. It's important, however, to be clear on what Swinburne really means by 'simplicity'. When theists claim God is simple, they don't mean that She lacks complex *functions*, but that God is simple in regard to Her *structure*. I doubt that such a response would move Dawkins; for Dawkins, we can imagine a whole host of creatures – ghosts, fairies and spaghetti monsters – who are no less simple than God. Did we not learn anything from Darwin? If we want the simplest explanation, let us look to the earth before the heavens.

Questions to consider

1. Is it wrong to indoctrinate children with religion?
2. Where would you place yourself on Dawkins's seven-point scale?
3. How credible is the multiverse theory as an explanation for fine-tuning?
4. Is the Bible just another work of fiction?
5. Should we treat theism as a scientific hypothesis?

Recommended reading

Advanced

Richard Dawkins, *The Blind Watchmaker: Why the Evidence of Evolution Reveals a Universe Without Design* (London: Penguin Books, 1986).

> For those looking for an engaging and elegant explanation of Darwinian evolution – and how it can account for the natural world's complexity – there is no better book than *The Blind Watchmaker*.

Richard Dawkins, *The Selfish Gene* (Oxford: Oxford University Press, 1976).

> *The Selfish Gene* established Dawkins as one of the century's leading biologists. The book's central thesis is that bodies are survival machines for self-replicated coded information (genes); genes, says Dawkins, are the primary units that evolution selects between.

Intermediate

Richard Dawkins, *The God Delusion* (London: Transworld, 2006).

> This book secured Dawkins's reputation as the world's most prominent atheist. The rhetoric is exciting in its own right, and there's a lot to be gained from his thoughts on religion's nature, origin and impact throughout the ages. If you want to know more about Dawkins's thoughts on any of the popular arguments for God – and why his views have stirred up so much controversy – then this is the place to go.

Richard Dawkins, *The Greatest Show on Earth: The Evidence for Evolution* (New York: Free Press, 2009).

> In his other books, Dawkins focuses on the *process* of evolution – how it functions and leads to complexity. In *The Greatest Show on Earth* he makes his explicit, systematic case for why evolution is true. In essence, the book's goal is to respond to the creationist's argument that evolution is 'only a theory'.

Beginner

Richard Dawkins, *Outgrowing God: A Beginner's Guide* (New York: Random House, 2019).

> Short and accessible, *Outgrowing God* is perfect for those who are new to Dawkins's brand of atheism. The book consists of two parts – God and evolution – in which Richard dismantles the argument from scripture and offers a compelling (and beautifully written) explanation of Darwinian evolution.

A. C. Grayling, *The God Argument: The Case Against Religion and For Humanism* (Bloomsbury: London, 2013).

> A. C. Grayling is another influential atheist; however, Grayling is a philosopher rather than a biologist. *The God Argument* is a short book that aims to address all the popular arguments for theism. Chapters Five and Six – on why atheism should be preferred over agnosticism – come highly recommended.

Chapter Seven

The Problem of Evil for Atheists

Yujin Nagasawa

Introduction

No life is free from evil. Whether it's the sting of a splinter, the slow burn of grief or the embarrassment of misspeelling a word, the reality of our suffering is undeniable. The existence of evil is typically presented as a reason for rejecting the existence of an all-loving God. 'If God really cared about us,' says the cynic, 'then She wouldn't have created a world containing hurricanes, hookworms and holocausts.' This argument – known as 'the problem of evil' – offers one of the most persuasive objections to theism. However, before we go tearing up our bibles and Qur'ans, we should ask whether this problem is unique to theism, or whether it applies to atheism as well.

In this chapter, we'll be discussing the problem of evil with one of philosophy of religion's most progressive and innovative thinkers, Professor Yujin Nagasawa. Leading several of world philosophy's largest research projects and institutions,[1] Nagasawa has inspired a tidal wave of new interest into alternative concepts of God and underrepresented religious traditions. As well as carving out new areas of scholarship, his work is precise, colourful and carries with it deep existential implications.

The argument presented in this chapter is no different. The physical world, says Nagasawa, is rotten to its core: the system that produces intelligent life has been grinding out pain and suffering for billions of years. Though Yujin accepts that this presents a challenge to traditional theism, he also maintains – quite uniquely – that the problem of evil poses a significant threat to atheism. In short, Nagasawa argues that it's unreasonable to believe that the world is a good place, as he says most atheists do, without blinding oneself to the violence and misery of the natural world. In fact, Nagasawa takes this a step further, arguing that the problem of evil is a bigger danger to atheism than it is to theism. If he's right, then the existence of evil may give us reason to embrace God, rather than abandon Her.

Systemic evil

Whether it's being buried in an avalanche or enduring one of Sandra Bullock's movies, we all know what evil is; but what does it mean to describe something as 'evil'?

We typically use the word 'evil' to refer to things that cause undesired pain or suffering. When a person experiences toothache or mourns the death of a loved one, they encounter the reality of evil – it's something that we're all deeply familiar with. Philosophers have spent a long time worrying about evil and they've come up with a distinction between two different types. The first type is 'moral evil': these are negative states of affairs that are caused freely and directly by human beings. Unfortunately, we're never short of examples: starting wars, kicking dogs and domestic abuse are all forms of moral evil. Of course, many undesirable events aren't caused by humans – plagues, hurricanes, bear attacks and the like – and these fall into a second category: 'natural evil'.

In addition to natural and moral evils, I argue that there's also a third type – what I call 'systemic evil'. Systemic evil consists of the pain and suffering that is caused by natural selection, the mechanism that underpins the process of evolution. This mechanism dictates that in order to survive creatures must fight and kill one another for the world's limited resources. It's a cruel, blind process that favours the selfish and ensures that the weak are eliminated. This tragedy has been playing out for billions of years, and it's the very system that brings us here today. Our lives are only possible because of the pain and suffering of our ancestors.

If 'natural evil' refers to all the undesirable events that aren't caused by humans, then isn't systemic evil just another type of natural evil?

You might think that systemic evil and natural evil are the same thing, but they're actually quite different. In the case of systemic evil, we're not talking about *specific* natural events like the Iran Blizzard or the Haiti Earthquake; nor are we talking about *types* of natural events like cancers or famines. Those are all forms of natural evil. When we're considering systemic evil, we're referring to the entire system that underpins our existence. 'Systemic evil' refers to the mechanism *that is* evolution and, in that sense, is much deeper than the other types discussed in philosophy.

As you know, natural and moral evil are usually counted as evidence against the existence of God. Does the same apply to systemic evil?

It certainly does. The problem of systemic evil is a great challenge for theists. To understand why, consider the following example. Suppose I filled a cage with lots of different animals – lions, lizards, leopards and the like – and a small amount of food and water. If I were to lock the cage and watch these animals fight for their survival, you would think I was playing an extremely horrible game! Yet, this is the state of the natural world. The challenge for theists is to explain how this situation is compatible with a morally perfect God.

Existential optimism

This looks like a serious objection. Do you think this problem is unique to theism?

Before I answer, I'd like to introduce a position called 'existential optimism'. Existential optimism claims that the world is, overall, a good place and that we should be happy and pleased to be alive. I would say that most people are existential optimists, regardless of whether they're atheists or theists. 'Sure, the world isn't perfect,' they say, 'and terrible things happen all the time. But overall it's a good place and I'm grateful to be here.' It turns out that systemic evil isn't just a problem for theists but atheists as well because atheists – as I have said – are usually optimists.

Natural selection necessitates the pain and suffering of the world's creatures – a system on which human beings are <u>nomologically dependent</u> – so how can we say that we're happy to be alive and that the world is a great place when it's systemically evil? Existential optimism is *incompatible* with systemic evil! This is what I call the 'existential problem of systemic evil', and it's a problem for both theists and atheists.

Nomological laws are, in essence, fundamental laws of nature. Here, Nagasawa makes the (uncontroversial) claim that natural selection is one such law, on which the evolution of human beings depends. In fact, all living organisms are <u>nomologically dependent</u> on natural selection.

Okay, so let's accept (for now) that there's a tension between systemic evil and believing that the world is a good place. I'm worried, however, that you might be putting words into the atheist's mouth. Do atheists *really* believe that the world is 'good'?

I think they do. Atheists are often characterized as these gloomy pessimists who aren't very happy with the world, but I don't think that's right. In fact, I would say that most atheists are happy people who embrace existential optimism. To take one example, Richard Dawkins thinks we should be grateful to be born out of evolution.[2]

What makes you think that Dawkins is an optimist?

Well, let me quote him directly. I think this captures his view quite nicely:

> When I lie on my back, look up at the Milky Way on a clear night and see the vast distances of space and reflect that these are also vast distances of time as well, when I look at the Grand Canyon and see the strata going down, down, down through periods of time which the human mind can't comprehend, I'm overwhelmingly filled with a sense of almost worship. . . . It's a feeling of sort of abstract gratitude that I am alive to appreciate these wonders.[3]

It's a beautiful sentiment, in which Dawkins is clearly expressing his belief that the world is a good place and that he is grateful for his existence. That's existential optimism!

Maybe Dawkins can sidestep this problem. For example, perhaps he could denounce the reality of objective moral truths in favour of <u>non-cognitivism</u>. Rather than saying it's *true* that the world is good, he might say that his gratitude is simply an expression of emotion.

He might say that, but I think this raises further problems. First of all, if ethical statements don't have any truth value, then atheists can't present the problem of evil against theism: you can't say that God is incompatible with the world if 'the world is evil' isn't *true*. This is because non-cognitivists deny the existence of

> One version of <u>non-cognitivism</u> (known as 'emotivism') claims that instead of referring to moral facts about the world, ethical statements only express how people feel. On this view, declaring that 'murder is wrong' is equivalent to moaning, 'Boo, I don't like murder!'

objective moral facts – that statements such as 'murder is wrong' are *true* or *false* – and, therefore, moral statements can't conflict with claims that *are* true or false, such as 'God exists'. The thrust of the problem of evil is that the statements that God exists and that evil exists cannot be both true. However, if, as non-cognitivism says, the latter statement is neither true nor false, then the problem of evil does not arise in the first place.

What if atheists said, '*Theists* believe in moral truth, systemic evil and a morally perfect God, but these beliefs are inconsistent!', without holding any of these beliefs themselves?

I think that's a better way of formulating the problem of evil; however, this raises another problem. As we've seen, existential optimists claim that 'the world is a good place' and, therefore, the atheist who accepts existential optimism is making a moral judgement about the world. In short: if you're a non-cognitivist, then you can't say that it's *true* that the world is good. We should also keep in mind that atheists want to say things like 'suffering is bad' and 'we shouldn't harm the innocent'. If these are just expressions of emotions or preferences, then these claims have no real substance to them. Put it this way, for the non-cognitivist, thinking that *we shouldn't torture children* is the same as believing *we shouldn't watch Sandra Bullock's movies*: although atheists will agree that both experiences are bad, they will want to say that these are very different kinds of statements; I doubt that many atheists would be happy to say these beliefs carry the same weight.

The big picture

If you're right, and most atheists are existential optimists who believe in objective moral truths, are there any significant implications?

I think there are, yes. We typically take it for granted that the problem of evil provides a reason to give up theism for atheism. However, I think it's the other way around. To understand why, let's take a look at the metaphysical systems of these two views. Atheists are usually naturalists, so they think that the material world is all that exists. On the other hand, theists are typically supernaturalists, which means they believe in a reality beyond the material world. For theists, this supernatural reality includes heaven, as well as entities like God and His angels.

This leads us to the crux of my argument. While atheists must accept that the world is, overall, a bad place, theists can appeal to the goodness of the supernatural world, and that gives them a significant advantage over atheists. This means that theists, who (overwhelmingly) believe that the world is good, can point to God and heaven and say, 'There's a significant amount of good that lies beyond the physical world and, therefore, we don't have to accept that the world is (on the whole) evil.'

To illustrate the point, I'd like you to imagine a canvas – a painting of the world that hangs in the home of our existential optimist. On this canvas, all of the positive things in the world are painted yellow, and all of the negative things are painted grey. Of course, when asked by an overly inquisitive guest, the optimist accepts that the canvas has some grey bits. 'But, overall,' they explain, 'it's yellow.' Interested to learn more about their prized possession, suppose our optimist asks a radiographer to inspect the painting. After scanning beneath the painting's surface, the radiographer turns to them and says: 'Actually, if you look at the underpainting, this painting's mostly grey!'

And this grey underpainting is a metaphor for the world's systemic evil?

Exactly! Now, if the optimist is an atheist, then they have to accept the radiographer's judgement that the painting is mostly grey. Why? Because atheists think that the material world is all that exists. However, for the theist, reality contains more than one dimension. Rather than being a single canvas, they believe that the world is a diptych: it includes a second canvas! This second canvas – which includes illustrations of heaven, God and His angels – is all yellow. It's this second canvas that allows theists to say that the world is mostly yellow rather than mostly grey. So, unlike the atheist, the theist can maintain their optimism.

Perhaps the optimistic atheist could offer a solution; if they were to explain why natural selection isn't as bad as we think it is, would that level the playing field?

It might level the playing field, but the theist will always hold the advantage. Suppose that you're right, and atheists can come up with a good response to the problem of systemic evil. Now, if the solution can be found within nature, then theists can appeal to the same response because their <u>ontology</u> – like the atheist's – includes the material world. In

> The branch of metaphysics known as '<u>ontology</u>' aims to identify the various categories of existence. In other words, ontology focuses on what *types* of things exist.

that case, we have a draw. However, if atheists can't respond to the problem of systemic evil, then theism holds a significant advantage over atheism: theists can appeal to their second canvas. Therefore, the atheist can only draw or lose, but the theist will always draw or win!

Do you think that the atheist *could* draw? For example, could they argue that the products of evolution (happy, intelligent creatures) are worth the pain and suffering that got them here?

I don't think this suggestion, that the fruits of evolution are worth the suffering, is successful. It's similar to greater good theodicies in response to the traditional problem of evil. According to this view, certain evils are necessary for realizing some greater good; however, it cannot be that *all* instances of evil are necessary for realizing greater good. There are many instances of gratuitous or pointless evil in the world.

> The word 'theodicy' means 'justifying God'. According to greater good theodicies, we should prefer to live in a world with evil than without it, because evil allows for higher-order goods such as free will and the opportunity to develop our characters.

The second canvas

Earlier in our discussion, you said it would be 'extremely horrible' to create a system of natural selection. Doesn't this still reflect very badly on God's character?

Perhaps at face value, but for the theist there is plenty of good (such as the infinite goodness of heaven) beyond the natural world and that's a powerful reason for maintaining the belief that God is good.

I'm concerned that the supernatural world isn't as good as you're making out. After all, don't theists also believe in hell – a place of infinite suffering! Does the infinite suffering of hell not counterbalance the infinite goodness of heaven?

The simple answer is that it depends on what you think about hell. If you believe that hell is a place where people are tortured for all of eternity, in which hell contains an infinite number of horrible things, then yes: I can see how appealing to the second canvas won't benefit the theist. However, I would say that most theists reject this simplistic picture of the afterlife. They say that hell is not a place where people are tortured, but where people are detached from God. If you accept this view, then you reject the idea that there's a place of infinite suffering and this allows theism to maintain its advantage.

I can't help but think that the theist's advantage is somewhat superficial. Don't they need to show that there *is* a second canvas – that the supernatural world exists – before they appeal to it?

I don't want to argue that theism is true or false, my point is simply that theism has the better ontology. But I'll take your point. To defend their advantage, theists will have to supplement their belief in the supernatural by providing reasons for thinking that reality extends beyond the natural world. My favourite method of doing so is the modal ontological argument, which argues that a morally perfect God *must* exist. Critics often say that arguments for theism might be very clever, but that they could never persuade atheists to convert to theism. I don't think that's true. In fact, it was the ontological argument that inspired my own conversion from atheism to theism. So, in answer to your question: I think there are good reasons for believing there's a second canvas.

If you're way up in the heavens, you've got a long way to fall

One popular response to the world's ills can be found in the work of <u>Albert Camus</u>, who retells the Greek <u>myth of King Sisyphus</u>. The gods – who punish Sisyphus for his attempts to cheat death – force him to roll a boulder up and down a hill for all of eternity. Instead of falling into pessimism, Camus tells us that the struggle towards the heavens 'is enough to fill a man's heart' and that we must 'imagine Sisyphus happy'.[4] In other words, even though the world is a bad place, like Sisyphus, we can find happiness. What do you make of this response?

> <u>Albert Camus</u> (1913–1960) was a philosopher and novelist. Awarded the Nobel Prize in Literature, Camus's work explored the tension between humanity's desire for meaning and the world's indifference to our existence.

I think it's important that we distinguish between *solutions* and *responses* here. On the one hand, *solutions* to the problem will argue that the world isn't as bad as we think it is (typically by appealing to greater goods); whereas *responses* accept that the world is systemically evil and tell us how we can deal with it. Many theistic solutions to the problem of evil are unsatisfying because they attempt to explain evil away, but Camus faces the evil. He doesn't deny its reality! Instead, he tries to figure out what he could do in *response* to the world's evil! Rather than being an optimist, it looks like Camus is saying that we should be pessimists who strive to live with the absurdity of life in an authentic way. If that's right, then the problem of evil for atheists doesn't apply to Camus because he doesn't think the world is a good place.

The myth of King Sisyphus

I like this comparison with Camus because it touches on another important issue. For Camus, the greatest philosophical question was whether the atheist's life can be meaningful. But, interestingly, William Lane Craig has argued that if God doesn't exist and life ends at death, then it has no ultimate purpose or significance[5] – which is essentially what Camus thought. However, because Craig is a theist, he doesn't embrace pessimism: he can be hopeful that the world extends beyond the physical! My thoughts on the matter are similar. If you think that there's something beyond nature, then life has meaning, and you can embrace existential optimism. Again, it looks like the atheist is at a disadvantage.

Suppose that on his way up the hill, somebody greets Sisyphus with a Terry's Chocolate Orange.[6] He unravels its vibrant orange wrapper, and he's happy and pleased that he can enjoy one of life's greatest pleasures despite his wider suffering. Is this a case of reasonable optimism?

I think so, yes. But remember, just because Sisyphus enjoys his Terry's Chocolate Orange, and quite rightly so, this doesn't eradicate systemic evil. Sisyphus accepts that systemic evil and existential optimism are incompatible, but he decides to take a positive attitude towards his situation. Fundamentally,

A delicious combination of cocoa and orange oil make Terry's Chocolate Orange© the perfect stocking filler.

Sisyphus is an existential pessimist: the world is mostly grey, but it has a few yellow (and in this case orange) aspects too.

If you're right and it's unreasonable for atheists to think that the world is a good place, why do you think so many of them are optimists?

One promising explanation for this might be found in evolution itself. Perhaps our pessimistic ancestors weren't quite as motivated as their optimistic cousins and those who saw the world as a good place, and were grateful to live in it, had a stronger motivation to survive. Optimists are known to be generally healthier, happier and more productive. Some scientists even argue that a population tends to be optimistic over time because overconfidence maximizes the fitness of individuals.[7]

It seems like the stakes aren't quite as high for the atheist who, except for being plunged into a gloomier existence, can give up their optimism and nothing really changes! Do you think that theists, who spend their lives worshipping God, have more to lose?

In one sense, you're right. It's much easier for atheists to give up on their optimism. Facing the problem of systemic evil, they could accept existential pessimism and that would make their worldview consistent. It's the sort of thing Camus and Sisyphus were doing and, ultimately, I think that's what they should do. On the other hand, theism says that God created a good and beautiful world; so yes, the stakes are probably higher for the theist. With that said, the good news for theists is that they have an *infinite* number of resources at their disposal; theists can argue that the world is, in fact, good. But how can an atheist stand on the bones of countless intelligent creatures – animals who died painfully and miserably – and proclaim that we should be happy and pleased to live in such a cruel and violent world? The costs that these animals paid for our survival seem unjustifiably high. Atheists must give up their optimism. They don't have a choice.

Afterthoughts

Whatever you make of Nagasawa's argument, one can't deny its ingenuity. For centuries, atheists have argued that God's goodness can't be reconciled with the world's evils, without asking whether this presents a challenge to their own worldview. If he's right, it looks like atheists have a big problem on their hands.

Before we accept that atheists face the problem, however, we should question Yujin's claim that most people are existential optimists. I suspect that atheists – in particular, Dawkins and his followers – would accept that the natural world is a bad place but insist that they should, nevertheless, be grateful for their lives. I don't think this is an inconsistent position to hold. To understand why, consider the following example. Suppose that you find yourself at the mercy of a natural disaster – a colossal hurricane which tears through your neighbourhood for months on end. Once the dust finally settles, you would undoubtedly express your happiness and gratitude for life. After all, you have defeated incredible odds! I think it would be uncharitable for us to judge your expression – 'I'm so happy to be alive!' – as an endorsement of existential optimism. Instead, if we sat down over a coffee, you would probably explain how you believe that the natural world is fundamentally evil, that you have experienced great loss and suffering, but that *you* are grateful to have escaped the bloody clutches of nature. Perhaps the same is true of Dawkins and his followers: they are not optimists, but pessimists who are grateful for their existence.

I don't think that this would concern Yujin too much, who would insist that systemic evil is a significant problem for the world's optimistic atheists. On this point, I think Nagasawa is right. If the atheist *were* to endorse the central claim of existential optimism – that the world is, on the whole, a good place – then the hell-denying theist will find themselves with a significant advantage. If there's a lesson to this chapter, it's this: if you're an atheist, then you have to accept that the world is a bad place.

Questions to consider

1. Is the physical world systemically evil?
2. What does it mean to say, 'the world is a good place'?
3. Can we accept that the canvas is grey yet maintain that we're grateful to be alive?
4. Is the problem of evil a bigger problem for theism or atheism?
5. If hell is a place of infinite suffering, what are the implications for theism?

Recommended reading

Advanced

Yujin Nagasawa, *Maximal God: A New Defence of Perfect Being Theism* (Oxford: Oxford University Press, 2017).

Yujin develops an unorthodox version of perfect-being theology – which defines God as the greatest metaphysically possible being – before arguing for God's necessary existence through the modal ontological argument. This text is for anybody interested in the concept of God and why Nagasawa converted from atheism to theism.

David Benatar, *Better Never to Have Been: The Harm of Coming into Existence* (Oxford: Oxford University Press, 2006).

In this popular book, the (pessimistic) atheist David Benatar argues that, given the state of the natural world, it is morally wrong to bring more life into the existence. Once you've read the book, it's worth checking out Nagasawa's response to Benatar.[8]

Intermediate

Yujin Nagasawa, 'The Problem of Evil for Atheists', in *The Problem of Evil: Eight Views in Dialogue*, ed. Nick Trakakis (Oxford: Oxford University Press, 2018), 151–63.

This is the text that we discussed in the interview. Nagasawa outlines the systemic problem of evil and why atheists (but not theists) must abandon existential optimism.

Janna Thompson, 'The Apology Paradox', in *Philosophical Quarterly*, vol. 50, no. 201 (2001): 470–5.

In this short, engaging paper, Thompson discusses the conflict between our gratitude for life and the suffering of our ancestors. While Yujin is concerned with the biological system which governs the natural world, Thompson asks what it means for those in positions of privilege to apologize for historical injustices.

Beginner

David Benatar, 'Kids? Just Say No', *Aeon*, October 2017, www.aeon.co/essays/having-children-is-not-life-affirming-its-immoral.

In this profound and powerfully argued article, Benatar explains how all human beings are perpetrators of evil and why this means that we should stop having children.

Kola Abimbola, 'God and Evil', *Philosophy Now*, 1993, www.philosophynow.org/issues/8/God_and_Evil.

If you're new to the problem of evil, this is a great place to start. Abimbola discusses the classic problem of evil and evaluates some of the popular responses that have been offered in defence of God.

Chapter Eight

The Evil-God Challenge

Stephen Law

Introduction

The problem of evil is perhaps the most powerful argument against classical monotheism. However, as Nagasawa pointed out in our previous chapter, religious believers claim to have an infinite number of resources at their disposal; resources which, they say, can be used to explain why God allows evil to exist. A lot of ink has been spilt on whether these explanations are successful. It's a complex and contentious debate, which rarely leads to opponents changing their minds. Perhaps, if we want to break the deadlock between theists and atheists, we need to reframe the discussion.

In 2010, Stephen Law released a paper that would do just that. Today, Law's article – 'The evil-god challenge' – is among philosophy of religion's most downloaded and discussed papers of the past decade. It's hard to overstate its impact. Law's work – through books, videos, podcasts and live events – has a global audience in the millions and has attracted the attention of some of the world's most notable religious philosophers.

The evil-god challenge can be stated as follows: why is believing in a good god significantly more reasonable than believing in an evil god? Fundamentally, this question depends on the truth of what Law calls the 'symmetry thesis', which states that the two beliefs – belief in good god or evil god – are roughly as reasonable. To reject the symmetry thesis, religious believers need to explain why belief in a good god is significantly more reasonable than belief in its malevolent counterpart. If they can't do this, says Law, then traditional theism is scarcely more reasonable than belief in an evil god, which is nothing short of absurd.

The challenge

One of your arguments against god's existence, 'the evil-god challenge', has received enormous amount of attention. Who is this 'evil god' and how are they a challenge to theism?

According to most Christians, Jews and Muslims, there exists one god who is all-powerful, all-knowing and maximally good. Religious believers give lots of reasons for thinking that this god – let's call them 'good god' – exists. For example, some argue that the universe's existence and finely tuned character point towards a supremely intelligent creator. Let's say, just for a moment, that their arguments have some credibility. (I don't think they're credible, but let's just pretend they are.) Now, I want you to consider an alternative hypothesis. Imagine a similar god who differs in one crucial respect: rather than being maximally good, this being is maximally evil. That's what I mean by 'evil god'. The first thing to notice is that many of the arguments used to support a good god, such as the universe's existence and fine-tuned character, can also be used to support an evil god. In fact, I think that once we consider all of the arguments and evidence at our disposal, we'll find that the likelihood of both hypotheses – good god and evil god – is fairly similar. In other words, I think there's a rough symmetry between the two hypotheses. I call this the 'symmetry thesis'.

Now, here's the problem. The evil-god hypothesis is obviously ridiculous. If a grown-up told you they believed in an evil god, you might question their sanity. However, according to the symmetry thesis, believing in good god is no more reasonable than believing in evil god. So, if the good-god hypothesis is roughly as reasonable as the evil-god hypothesis – and believing in an evil god is absurd – then we ought to think that believing in a good god is absurd as well. For the Abrahamic believer, the only way to avoid this conclusion is to answer the challenge. The challenge is, in essence, to explain why the symmetry thesis is false: what makes believing in good god *significantly* more reasonable than believing in evil god?

Why does one hypothesis need to be 'significantly' more reasonable than the other?

If one is downright ludicrous, then pointing out that the other one is *slightly* more reasonable is hardly good enough. Maybe believing there are fairies at the bottom of your garden is somewhat more reasonable than believing Santa delivers your presents on Christmas Day. The minor difference doesn't matter; both of these beliefs are absurd. That's why the theist needs a reason for thinking that the good-god hypothesis is *significantly* more reasonable.

Might they achieve this by appealing to the goods within the universe? For example, Abrahamic believers could argue that the world is not nearly evil enough to be the creation of such a malevolent deity?

This response, which I call the 'problem of good', says that we can reasonably rule out the existence of evil god because the world contains a very significant amount of good. Surely an evil god would not create a world with so much laughter and love, rainbows and contentment. Why, for example, does evil god allow us to help each other and reduce the suffering of others? Now, I accept that the problem of good is a strong enough reason to reject the evil-god hypothesis. Don't forget, however, that the world also contains a very significant amount of evil. This parallel argument, the notorious 'problem of evil', is just as big of a problem for the theist as it is the evil-god challenger. 'Why', asks the challenger, 'would good god create a world that contains so much pain and misery?' Consider all of the terrible things that we do to each other – murders, genocides, torture, cruelty, exploitation – and then there's all of the natural diseases, disasters and millions of years of animal suffering. For almost the entire sweep of human history, your chances of making it to adulthood were little better than fifty-fifty. Many of those children's deaths would have been slow and horrific, and then there's the psychological suffering of the parents. Ask any parent, 'What's the worst thing that could happen to you?', and they'll probably tell you it'd be watching their child die a slow and unpleasant death. If we can reasonably rule out the evil-god hypothesis because of the problem of good, and I think we can, then why can't we rule out the good-god hypothesis because of the problem of evil?

Theists have been responding to the problem of evil for centuries. Can't they overcome the challenge by appealing to theodicies and <u>defences</u>?

Yes, the good-god defender might appeal to theodicies and defences, but so can the evil-god challenger. Let's take an example. One of the most popular responses to the problem of evil is the free-will defence. According to this argument, good god permits evil to allow for the greater good of free will. If good god had created humans as puppets who always did the right thing, then we wouldn't be morally responsible for our

> Theodicies try to explain *the* reasons for why God allows for evil. Alternatively, <u>defences</u> – more modestly – only offer *possible* reasons for why God allows for evil.

actions. Therefore, good god cut our strings and set us free. Sometimes we do the wrong thing, but if we weren't free, then good god would miss out on the tremendous good that is the human capacity to perform genuinely virtuous actions.

The problem with this kind of response is that it appears to work more or less equally effectively in defence of evil god. Answering the problem of good, the challenger can argue that evil god allows some people to be virtuous, but that's the price evil god pays for free will and genuinely malevolent actions. Evil god could have created us as puppets who always did wrong, but then we wouldn't be responsible for our actions. Therefore, to get the very worst kinds of evil – like freely chosen genocide and slavery – he cut our strings and set us free. Evil god allows for virtuous behaviour in order for us to be capable of horrendous moral depravity.

What about explanations of natural evil? The soul-making theodicy, for example, claims that evils which aren't caused by humans – such as hay fever and hurricanes – allow us to develop our characters. Can the challenger mirror this response?

I think they can. First, let's be clear on what the soul-making theodicy is supposed to show. As you say, according to theists, some of the evils in the universe allow us to develop our characters. Evil can help us grow and become better people. Call it a 'vale of soul-making'. As a parent, I taught my daughter to ride her bike. She didn't enjoy falling off and grazing her knees – children shed a lot of blood and tears when they're learning to ride a bike – but I encouraged her to keep trying. Why did I do that? Because that's how she'll grow as a person. She ought to learn the skill of riding a bike; she should learn how to overcome hardships and she'd benefit from the sense of achievement. According to the theist, the same is true for many of the evils in the natural world: the suffering that we go through in this life brings us closer to perfection. They give us opportunities. No pain, no gain.

> According to John Hick (1922-2012), the world is a vale of soul-making: the purpose of life on earth is for humans to become better people. Hick's argument, which finds its root in the work of Irenaeus (c. 130–202), continues to be popular among theists. In fact, Richard Swinburne made use of this argument in Chapter Two.

Notice, however, that with some minor adjustments, the challenger can use this same theodicy in response to the problem of good. 'Why', asks the theist, 'does evil god give us healthy young bodies that can ride bikes?' So he can take them away with age, of course. It's cruel to give something wonderful and then take it away – like giving a child a wonderful toy and then smashing it up in front of them. That makes the child more miserable than if they never had the toy to begin with. The same is true of our friends, children and all of our accomplishments. 'Why', asks the theist, 'did evil god give us children to love and to cherish?' Because it's only through loving our children that we can suffer the torment of evil god killing them on an industrial scale, as he has for hundreds of thousands of years. Love is required for the most appalling forms of psychological torment. This is not a vale of soul-making, but a vale of soul-destroying.

So, what are these reverse-theodicies supposed to show?

I'm trying to get the penny to drop. If you've spent a long time engaged in a certain kind of intellectual activity that's pretty flaky – but everyone around you is doing it, and everyone's telling you that it's pretty effective – then it can be hard to see that there's something suspect about the way you're thinking. The evil-god challenge is, in part, a way of getting theists to step outside of their skin and see what they're doing from a different perspective. Most of us can see immediately that, notwithstanding such ingenious mirror moves that might be used to defend belief in an evil god against the problem of good, it remains pretty obvious that (given observed goods) there's no evil god. If somebody used reverse-theodicies to defend belief in evil god, most theists would see through the charade. I'm asking them a question: why are your theodicies any better?

Breaking the symmetry

There are some theodicies that don't have obvious parallels. For example, Saint Augustine thought that evil entered the world when Adam and Eve committed the original sin and, therefore, good god isn't responsible for the world's evils.[1] It's difficult to imagine what a reverse-original sin would even look like. Does this difference, this *asymmetry*, offer a possible solution to the challenge?

It doesn't solve my version of the challenge, though it might be a problem for earlier versions. One of the earliest evil-god challenges appeared in Edward Madden and Peter Hare's book, *Evil and the Concept of God*.[2] For Madden and Hare, the problems of good and evil were 'completely isomorphic'.[3] In the 1970s, Stephen Cahn defended a similar view and,[4] in the 1990s, Edward Stein and Christopher New came to the same conclusion.[5] I disagree. Original sin is just one example of an explanation that doesn't have an obvious parallel. Remember, however, that I claimed that there is a *rough* symmetry between the reasonableness of the two hypotheses. This is different to what the earlier challengers thought. In assessing the reasonableness of each hypothesis we should look at *all* the available evidence and explanations for it. True, some defences of a good god might be less effective than defences of an evil god, and vice versa, and original sin is a good example of this; there is no obvious parallel. However, it's one of the least plausible theodicies that theists can offer. There was no Adam or Eve. In fact, we

> Saint Augustine of Hippo (354–430) had an enormous impact on Christian thought. In his autobiographical masterpiece, *Confessions* (397–400), Augustine shares a story in which he steals pears from a neighbour's orchard. 'My feasting', Augustine wrote, 'was *only* on the wickedness which I took pleasure in enjoying.' Reflecting on his experience, Augustine decided that he didn't enjoy pears, and that humans are born with a natural inclination to do evil.

> Following a biblical interpretation, our natural inclination towards evil is attributed to the Fall of Man. This event refers to Adam and Eve's original sin, in which they ate from 'the forbidden tree of the knowledge of good and evil'. Theologians continue to debate why God was so bad at naming trees.

now know that unimaginably vast quantities of pain and suffering stretch back millions of years before humans ever lived or sinned. So, yes, there's an asymmetry here – this theodicy doesn't flip – but that doesn't have much of an impact on the overall balance of reasonableness.

Are there any asymmetries that favour evil god over good god?

In think so. One candidate is the argument from religious experience, miracles, revelations and the like. People typically think that religious experiences and miracles are evidence for good god rather than evil god. A good god will want to cure us, alleviate suffering and reveal himself to us; an evil god wouldn't miraculously cure people. However, on closer examination, maybe this evidence better supports an evil god. The fact that the world's religions and denominations are so varied in their beliefs seems to be a bigger problem for the theist than it does for the challenger. If I were an evil god, I'd might well maximize evil by engaging in deception. I might dress up in a white outfit, throw on a halo and appear in the religious experiences of one group. I'd also perform some genuine miracles – which, being a god, I can do. Perhaps I'll tell them that Christianity is the one true religion and raise Jesus from the dead. Then, I would go to another group – still dressed in my good god garb – and tell them things that contradict my messages to the first group. For example, perhaps I'd perform some miracles but tell them that Jesus was *not* raised from the dead. Now each of these groups believes – because of the *genuine* miracles and so on – they have the one true god on their side, and that's a recipe for a deep and bloody conflict! An evil god would be delighted with that result! Surely a good god, on the other hand, would never reveal himself in such a misleading way, or allow such confusion to reign because of contradictory revelatory experiences, miracles and teachings. The question that we should ask ourselves is this: which of our two hypotheses is a better fit for the evidence? In my view, the distribution of religious miracles, experiences and scriptures looks like it offers more support to evil god than good god.

I wonder, is it even possible for a maximally perfect being to be evil rather than good?

I suppose there might be a logical problem with the idea of an evil god, just as some atheists think there's a logical problem with the idea of a good god. Critics have argued for a long time that god's various attributes can't be combined, or that god's individual attributes – such as god's omnipotence – generate contradictions. It may be that you can present similar objections against an evil god too. However, even if you could establish a logical problem when it comes to the idea of an evil god, we can still run the evil-god challenge. My argument is this: if you can reasonably reject the evil-god hypothesis because of the problem of good, and I think you can, then you can reasonably reject the good-god hypothesis because of the problem of evil. To point out that there are *further*, *logical* problems with the idea of an evil god is to miss the point. The evil-god challenge can still be used in this way, even if it turned out that the idea of an evil god is logically incoherent.

Perhaps the theist could claim that the world contains *significantly more good* than evil. If this were true, then the problem of good would rule out the evil-god hypothesis; however, the problem of evil wouldn't rule out good-god hypothesis. Is this a better response?

I don't think so. First, is there significantly more good than evil? It's very hard to quantify good and evil; I wouldn't be confident about the assessment that there's a lot more good than evil, or vice versa. As anyone that's watched a few nature documentaries will know, for many of the world's sentient inhabitants, life involves quite extraordinary amounts of suffering. Nature is cruel beyond our imagining. Moreover, it's also worth remembering that a mainstream Christian view is that the world is *absolutely saturated* in evil – every single human being is *so* morally depraved as to deserve everlasting torment. Second, even if it's true that there is significantly more good than evil, which I doubt, there can still be more than enough to rule out both god hypotheses. By comparison, you might suppose that there is ten times as much evidence against Santa than fairies. Clearly, however, there can still be more than enough evidence to rule out both. In fact, most theists acknowledge that the problem of evil is a very significant problem precisely because there's so much of it. They acknowledge that – on the face of it at least – it's hard to see how there could be a good god-justifying reason for every last ounce of it. If there's any pointless evil, even a teaspoonful, then there's no good god. Of course, the same is true of pointless good, an evil god won't permit any pointless goods – goods for which there's a more than adequate evil justification. Therefore, even if there is a significant asymmetry in terms of the amount of good and evil that exists, that needn't alter the fact that both hypotheses can reasonably be ruled on the basis of the distribution of observed good and evil.

What about the suggestion made by <u>sceptical theists</u>, that we are not in the position to know whether any evils are pointless? Sure there is pain, suffering and moral depravity but it may be that we can't think of a good-god-justifying reason for that evil. However, just because we can't think of such a reason doesn't mean a reason doesn't exist! Ultimately, we are mere humans, with limited intellectual abilities! Just as I shouldn't expect to

> According to <u>sceptical theists</u>, we can be confident that God exists; however, we should be sceptical about our ability to (fully) understand God's nature and motives.

be able to see an insect half a mile away, given my perceptual abilities, I shouldn't expect to be able to think of all the reasons good god might have for allowing for the existence of evil. For all we know, all evils are justified! Does this response tip the balance of reasonableness in favour of a good god?

No, because the exact same reasoning applies to evil god. Sceptical theism works just as well in defence of an evil god as it does for good god; after all, there could be evil reasons for the goods we observe, but we just can't think of them. In any case, I argue that sceptical theism is untenable. It generates other scepticisms that theists are unlikely to accept. For example, if sceptical theism is true, then for all I know there could be a good reason for why good god deceives me about the existence of the external world or the past. I can't reasonably assign a low probability to there being such reasons; however, if this were true, then I couldn't trust my senses or memory. For all I know, I'm being deceived! In

> According to Greek mythology, Zeus gave Pandora a <u>box</u> as a wedding present. Not knowing what it contained, Pandora opened her gift, which released a swarm of evil into the world: envy, pain, poverty, death and, worst of all, *Grown Ups 2* (2013).

short, sceptical theism opens a sceptical Pandora's <u>box</u>, with the scepticism spreading out in ways the theist is unlikely to accept.

William Lane Craig has offered an interesting response to your evil-god challenge. Craig thinks that your argument misses the point. Christians don't believe in god's goodness because of the goods they find in the world, he claims, but because 'being good' is what it *means* to be 'God'.

I think Craig has missed the point. I don't assume Christians make their case for good god based on observations of the world around them. Sure, the religious may sing songs about how everything's bright and beautiful, but most don't infer god's goodness from the goods in the world. I hope it's clear that my point is *not* that Christians *can't reasonably support* belief in a good god based on observed goods; rather, my argument is that if we *can reasonably reject* belief in an evil god based on observed goods, and I think we can, then we *can reasonably reject* belief in a good god based on observed evils. Craig seems to have misunderstood the challenge, which can be stated as follows: why can't we rule out both hypotheses based on observation of the world around us?

Well, let's consider another of Craig's responses. To run the evil-god challenge, you need to appeal to objective moral values. However, objective moral values, says Craig, can't exist unless there's a good god. Therefore, your challenge proves the very thing it sets out to disprove!

There are lots of Christian internet videos and posts making this same point: atheists can't use the problem of evil, since they don't believe in evil. As an atheist, if I admit evil exists, then I somehow admit that good god exists, because good and evil can only exist if good god exists. Of course, this objection relies on the thought that moral good and evil can't exist in the absence of god, which is highly dubious; even some theists deny that. However, in any case, this response to the problem rests on a misunderstanding. To run the problem of evil, atheists don't need to believe in evil. The point is that the problem of evil is an internal problem for theism. If a Christian thinks that pointless suffering – namely, good-god-*unjustified* suffering – is an evil, then given the existence of pointless suffering, they have a big problem. I can point out this problem even if I'm not committed to the existence of good, evil or god.

If we came up with a *really* powerful argument for good god – that could not be mirrored in favour of evil god – would that satisfy the challenger?

Given the compelling evidence against both evil god and good god, that argument will have to be very powerful. In order to make it reasonable to believe in a good god, given the problem of evil, any argument for a good god is going to have to be *really* strong; it's going to need to be a knock-out argument. The trouble is, however, that there are no such arguments. The most popular and intuitively appealing arguments for god aren't even arguments for a good god; they're merely arguments for a first cause, a necessary being, a prime mover or an intelligent designer. These arguments provide no clue as the moral attributes, if any, of the being that theists are arguing for. Considered in isolation, these arguments provide as much support for evil god as they do for good god; they do nothing to show that belief in a good god is significantly more reasonable than belief in an evil god.

Of course, there are some arguments specifically for a good god; however, they are among the weakest arguments for god's existence. For example, the moral argument for a good god, which Craig favours, is notoriously flimsy. Even Christian philosophers like Richard Swinburne reject it, although I know the argument plays well to lay audiences. Other arguments for good god – such as the argument that 'god as a perfect being requires moral perfection' – tend to be pretty abstract and slippery. Even among themselves, theists disagree about whether these arguments are any good, which suggests they're not that compelling. Moreover, these arguments can often be flipped in favour of an evil god. For example, just consider a reverse version of the ontological argument. The first premise states that *I can conceive of a maximally evil being*; the second premise maintains that *it is more evil for such a being to exist in reality than in my imagination*. The conclusion of such an argument would be that *a maximally evil being exists*. In summary, the case for a good god is *at best* pretty flimsy, and not nearly strong enough to outweigh the problem of evil.

The ghost of god

There are religious believers who argue that it's reasonable to believe in good god without evidence or argument. One such proponent, Alvin Plantinga, suggests we can come to know that god exists through our god-given sense, the _sensus divinitatis_. This sense, says Plantinga, provides direct, non-inferential knowledge of good god's existence. Might this be a way of unlocking the evil-god challenge?

In order to illustrate Plantinga's thinking, let's consider an example. Imagine that you're observing an apple in a bowl. It very much seems to you that there's an apple in the bowl – you can see it, feel it, smell it and taste it. Now, imagine if somebody were to offer you compelling evidence to the contrary. 'There is no apple in the bowl,' they explain, 'because there is a global shortage of apples and *no* apples have made their way to us here, in the UK.' You would think their argument was ridiculous; you can *directly observe* that there's an apple in the bowl. If, despite being careful, you nevertheless remain quite sure there's an apple

> The Latin phrase '*sensus divinitatis*' translates to 'sense of the divine'. Plantinga takes the concept from John Calvin (1509–1564), a central figure of the Protestant Reformation. According to Calvin, in addition to our five other senses, we also have a sixth sense: a sense of God. Our sense of God is a faculty of the mind – a natural instinct that reveals God's hand in the world.

present, then – despite the evidence that there are no apples in the UK – it can still be reasonable for you to believe there is an apple in front of you. I take that to be Plantinga's view, the religious person can insist that it can be reasonable for them to believe in the existence of good god, given that's very much how things seem to them, even if there's very strong evidence – such as all of the world's gratuitous evils – that there's no such god.

But isn't this an effective way of meeting the evil-god challenge? Can't direct religious experience trump the problem of evil?

Well, I think there are excellent grounds for being sceptical about such religious experiences. What would you think if I told you that, right now, my dead auntie was here in the room with us?

It depends on whether she's a corpse or a ghost.

She's a ghost.

I'd be relieved that she wasn't a corpse . . . but I'd still think you were crazy.

Exactly. It might really seem to me that my dead auntie is in the room with us, but, given other background information, it still isn't reasonable for me to believe it. Psychologists have pointed out that we human beings are horribly prone to false beliefs about extraordinary hidden agents. People believe in all sorts of thing – goblins, ghosts, fairies, angels and miraculous appearances of the Virgin Mary – on the basis of subjective experience and testimony. We know that very many of these beliefs are false. Indeed, they are constantly being debunked.[6] We are notoriously prone to such false positive beliefs, in which we think that there are extraordinary beings there when there are not. Psychological theories are now being developed to explain this striking tendency we have to over-detect agency.

Given this well-established tendency to think we are experiencing extraordinary hidden agency when we're not, it is not reasonable to trust our own experiences or reports of other peoples' experiences. This obviously extends to experiences of gods, including good god. It's reasonable to believe there's an apple in the bowl if that's very much how it seems to me – notwithstanding the evidence that there are no apples in the country – but it's no longer reasonable to trust appearance once I have grounds for thinking I'm hallucinating, being deceived by a hologram or in an environment where it's not uncommon for people to falsely report seeing apples. Under those circumstances, I have what philosophers call an 'undercutting defeater' for my belief. My belief there's an apple in the bowl could still be true, but it's no longer reasonable for me to hold that belief given this additional information. For much the same reason, it's no longer reasonable to trust experiences of god once we know they are a variety of experience notoriously prone to producing false positive beliefs.

Still, by appealing to good god, can't we explain a great deal of things that are otherwise deeply mysterious? Doesn't this count heavily in theism's favour?

I suspect this takes us close to the heart of the debate between atheists and theists. There's no doubt that if you posit an invisible being with supernatural powers you can explain all sorts of things and, with sufficient ingenuity, when somebody points out evidence against your belief in such beings, you can always explain away that evidence. Nine times out of ten, that's the theist's strategy: explain away the evidence and keep hammering away at the mysteries. Funnily enough, that's exactly how all sorts of conspiracy theories work. The same goes for belief in extraordinary supernatural beings such as fairies or gremlins. 'I can't find my keys! I thought I put them on the mantelpiece, but now they're here on the sofa.' Can you explain that? No you can't. It really is quite mysterious! But if I say that gremlins moved your keys – mischievous invisible creatures with supernatural powers – then I can explain what you cannot. Once I introduce an extraordinary hidden agent, I can explain anything I want. If you argue that there can't be any gremlins because we've never seen them, I can always cook up ways to explain that evidence away. We never see the gremlins because they're invisible or really good at hiding.

Rather than engaging in such make-believe, I think the right thing to do is be honest and admit we don't know the answers to all of these questions. I don't know how my keys ended up on the mantelpiece. Yes, gremlins would explain how they got there, but that doesn't give me much reason to believe in gremlins. Similarly, I don't know why the universe exists and I don't know how consciousness arises. Still, I can quite reasonably rule out the suggestion that evil god created the universe and conscious beings in order to torture them. If I can do that, then why can't I rule out good god on much the same basis? Surely I can. We may not know the answers to such deep philosophical questions, but that doesn't prevent us ruling out certain answers.

Afterthoughts

In my experience, the evil-god challenge never fails to inspire a passionate conversation. Whether it be a friend at a party or a professor at a conference, the idea of an evil god – and a new lens through which to explore the question of God's existence – seems to capture people's imaginations. Philosophically, the challenge's greatest asset is that it's indirect. Rather

than launching a head-on attack, Law points to evil god and says, 'Look how silly *that* belief is!' The theist laughs, but then Stephen turns to them and asks, 'What makes you think your belief is any different?'

In the wider literature, the evil-god challenge is treated as if it can be used to respond to *every* argument for God.[7] I don't think that's right. For example, theists have many reasons for thinking that god is good rather than evil. As Hill explained in our opening chapter, for example, the concept of God – namely, the greatest conceivable being – would possess every great-making property that it's possible to have. As moral goodness enhances greatness, but moral wickedness detracts from greatness, theists seem justified in attributing goodness (and not evil) to the greatest conceivable being. As we saw in his response to Craig, Law doesn't think this rebuttal applies to his version of the challenge. This is worth considering too. Law's version of the challenge rests on the claim that theists believe that evil god is absurd *because* of the problem of good. I wonder, however, whether this is something they actually believe. Do religious believers reject the evil-god hypothesis because the world contains so much good? If *that* is not their reason, then perhaps they can free themselves from the clutches of the challenge.

Questions to consider

1. Could an evil god have created the world?
2. How strong is the symmetry between the problem of good and the problem of evil?
3. Are religious experiences better evidence for evil god than good god?
4. When, if ever, is it reasonable to believe in invisible beings with supernatural powers?
5. Is the good-god hypothesis more reasonable than the evil-god hypothesis?

Recommended reading

<u>Advanced</u>

John Collins, 'The evil-god challenge: extended and defended', *Religious Studies*, vol. 55, no. 1 (2019): 85–109.

Collins's paper develops further symmetries between the good-god hypothesis and evil-god hypothesis. He also addresses those who have responded to Law's challenge, maintaining that each fails to overcome the symmetry thesis.

Christopher Weaver, 'Evilism, Moral Rationalism and Reasons Internalism', *International Journal for Philosophy of Religion*, vol. 77, no. 1 (2015): 3–24.

There are many papers responding to the evil-god challenge; this is one of the best. Weaver argues that, following certain metaethical assumptions, it would be impossible for an evil god to exist.

Intermediate

Stephen Law, 'The evil-god challenge', *Religious Studies*, vol. 46, no. 3 (2010): 353–73.

This is Stephen's landmark paper on the evil-god challenge: he introduces the challenge, compares it to previous versions and addresses a series of responses. If you enjoyed this chapter, then this is obligatory reading.

Stephen Law, *Believing Bullshit: How Not to Get Sucked into an Intellectual Black Hole* (New York: Prometheus Books, 2011).

In this short and accessible book, Stephen exposes fallacious ways of thinking and how we can respond to them. Law's focus isn't just religion but the techniques used by a range of dangerous belief systems.

Beginner

Asha Lancaster-Thomas, 'The Evil-god Challenge Part I: History and Recent Developments', *Philosophy Compass*, vol. 13, no. 7 (2018): 1–8.

For those looking to engage with the wider evil-god literature, this is a great place to start. Lancaster-Thomas discusses the history of the challenge, its nature – including a synopsis of the different types of evil-god challenges – and several arguments to which the challenge can be applied.

Asha Lancaster-Thomas, 'The Evil-God Challenge Part II: Objections and Responses', *Philosophy Compass*, vol. 13, no. 8 (2018): 1–10.

> This is the follow-up piece to the previous recommendation, in which Lancaster-Thomas gives an overview of different responses to the challenge. Lancaster-Thomas also discusses the strengths of the challenge and its implications for theism more generally.

Chapter Nine

Breaking the Spell

Daniel Dennett

Introduction

Does religion poison everything? Having read the chapters from Blackmore and Dawkins, you would be forgiven for thinking that it does. We would do well to remember, however, that the history of religion is one of change. If you were born in Ancient Greece, the gods would have brought you a great deal of suffering. Demanding sacrifices, enacting sexual violence and inflicting natural disasters, they were a selfish and unjust family who, despite your best efforts, could not be appeased. An all-forgiving father, on the other hand – one who will reward you with eternal life in heaven – is a very different matter. As time moves forward, so too does religion. The culture, metaphysics and ethics of belief have evolved significantly, and this evolution has ensured its survival. In the new age of science and reason, however, how (and whether) religion will continue to survive is another matter.

In this chapter, we'll be speaking to one of the world's most influential opponents of religious belief, Daniel Dennett, Professor of Philosophy at Tufts University. Dennett – alongside Richard Dawkins, Christopher Hitchens and Sam Harris – holds the menacing title of being one of the 'four horsemen of new atheism'. Alongside his fellow horsemen, Dennett is responsible for transforming atheistic philosophy into the worldview we are familiar with today.

Christopher Hitchens (1949–2011) was a journalist and author whose work focused on politics, literature and philosophy. Hitchens believed – as he put it in the subtitle of his bestselling book *God is Not Great* (2007) – that 'religion poisons everything'.

In many ways, Dennett's view isn't as radical as some of the other atheists we've encountered. Sure, his style of philosophy is unforgiving, yet his explanation of whether religion is a force for good or evil is – despite his apocalyptic title – surprisingly balanced. According to Dennett, like everything else that nature produces, religion is subject to evolution. Either religions adapt or they disappear. In either case, people come to understand that our understanding of the world and our responsibilities towards the people around us should be grounded in the natural rather than the supernatural.

Unreasonable belief

Let's get straight to the heart of the matter: do you think that believing in God is unreasonable?

Believing in God is completely unreasonable. I'm sure that many people will take offence when I say that, but how they feel about the matter has nothing to do with the likelihood of God's existence. Many sheltered people are, in one way or another, prevented from learning about the natural world and I think they can be forgiven for believing in God. With that said, for those of us who have access to the proper education, we have no excuse. When it comes down to it, believing in God is about as reasonable as believing in the Easter Bunny.

Religious philosophers have spent a lot of time trying to prove just the opposite. To take one example, Alvin Plantinga has argued that theists don't need arguments to justify their belief in God. Instead, they are warranted in holding their belief because God's existence is revealed to them through the *sensus divinitatis*, which forms the backdrop to his <u>Reformed epistemology</u>. This marks a clear difference between God and the Easter Bunny; billions of people have formed a natural belief in God, but very few people believe in the Easter Bunny! What do you make of this response?

> Epistemology is the study of knowledge: what knowledge is and how we acquire it. According to Plantinga's <u>Reformed epistemology</u>, just as taste justifies your belief that 'Marmite is delicious', your *sensus divinitatis* ('sense of the divine') justifies your belief that 'God is watching me'.

Well, I did say that belief in God and the Easter Bunny were 'about' as reasonable; of course, there are some minor differences. The first thing to say is that although lots of people believe in God, it's important that our beliefs aren't defined by other people's feelings on the matter, regardless of how many people think we're wrong. Truth is separate from people's thoughts and feelings. If millions of people started believing in the Easter Bunny, would that make that belief more reasonable?

Plantinga's claim that we have a 'sense of the divine' and that belief in God is 'properly basic' is ludicrously simple-minded. Isn't it funny that Plantinga has discovered that it is *his* God who has given him a 'divine sense'? What about Allāh? What about Vishnu? What about Zeus? By his own reasoning, belief in these gods should be considered just as reasonable as belief in the Christian God. This is Exhibit A of how religious belief can disable a philosopher. In reality, there are perfectly good naturalistic explanations for why people believe in God. Suppose I held the properly basic belief that 'Professor Plantinga is deluded'. I find that just as compelling and obvious as the belief that there's a cup in front of me. If I can't play that card, then Plantinga can't play his card.

Suppose the theist gave up on Reformed epistemology. Do you have any sympathy for those who claim that everybody is entitled to their own beliefs, even if their beliefs can't be fully justified?

There is a sense in which you're entitled to your own beliefs but not your own facts. However, in the case of religion, and any other case where beliefs influence actions, we should be reluctant to apply this rule of thumb. I think you can be criticized, and be morally culpable, for having wilfully ignorant beliefs. Ignorant beliefs can lead you to do all sorts of dreadful things – things that cause significant harm when you should have known better. Consider the old line, 'I didn't know the gun was loaded.' When it comes to religion, you're not entitled to believe that the gun isn't loaded. Religion has too much of an impact on people's lives. The only things people should be able to have blind faith in are those that have zero implications on how they behave. If somebody wants to believe that somewhere in outer space there is a massive ball of solid metal with the letters 'G O G' stamped on it, then that's fine by me. People are entitled to believe in Gog because it makes no difference. Similarly, if you wanted to use the word 'Gog' to describe the universe and its laws – rather than an all-powerful creator – then that's fine too. It's a label that won't make a difference. Albert Einstein thought something similar.[1] I wouldn't

> Albert Einstein (1879–1955) thought that God and the world were indistinguishable. This was in keeping with the pantheistic view of Baruch Spinoza (1632–1677). In Einstein's own words, 'I believe in Spinoza's God, Who reveals Himself in the lawful harmony of the world, not in a God who concerns Himself with the fate and the doings of mankind.'

describe the universe as 'God' myself, but I can see how using the term might offer a helpful way of capturing the awe one feels when marvelling about the size and complexity of the universe.

Outdated arguments

Over the past two thousand years, lots of arguments have appeared which, proponents say, show that God exists. One such argument, known as the 'ontological argument', claims to demonstrate God's existence with one hundred per cent certainty. According to this argument, because God is by definition a 'necessary' being, She must exist in every possible world. So long as God's existence is possible – for example, the concept of God does not contain any logical contradictions – then God's existence is actual. How would you respond to this argument?

I would stifle a yawn ... then I would say, 'Give me a break! The description of God as omnipotent, omniscient and all-loving is so obviously contradictory that it's hopeless.' In a certain sense, the gods of early religions were far more reasonable than the God of Abraham because they were so flawed. When religious institutions came along with their strong desire to have the 'correct' doctrine, they wanted to iron out all of these imperfections. Theologians started to turn the crank by claiming that God was perfect: 'My God is infinite!', 'My God is infinitely infinite!', 'My God is super infinitely infinite!' It was just silly. Ontological arguments are little more than intellectual playthings. Still, they're not that interesting.

If we're playing the game of philosophy, then we can't deny the conclusion of an argument without rejecting its structure or premises. With this in mind, if the theist could show that the concept of God was coherent, do you think that the ontological argument would prove that God exists?

I think this phrase that you used, 'the game of philosophy', is a nice way of putting it. A lot of the time philosophers are basically just playing tennis. One comes up with a formulation, and they write it down on a pad of paper. They've started the game with a proposition: can anybody refute it? Then, the ball is in the opponent's court, and they come up with a response or counterexample. Now there's a rally starting! The problem is that after a bit of back and forth the two players can blinker themselves and forget about whether the game is making any sense. That's precisely what's happened with the ontological argument.

Since the days of Socrates, philosophers have been going back and forth trying to discover the <u>essence</u> of abstract concepts like love, justice and knowledge. This demand on philosophers to define things in terms of their imagined essences with clear and unmovable boundaries has wasted a lot of time. If you're going to talk about essences, you're playing an antique game that deserves to go extinct. Arguments like the ontological argument play almost no role anywhere else in human enquiry because people recognize that meanings aren't essences. That's where the argument goes wrong: it asks us to talk meaningfully about God's essence, but this is impossible.

> In essence (sorry), an '<u>essence</u>' refers to a set of properties that are fundamental to an entity. For example, ontologically speaking, if a bicycle didn't have any wheels, then it wouldn't be a bicycle.
>
> Here, Dennett is claiming that there is no threshold at which an entity can be said to have acquired enough properties for it to be considered '*one of those entities*'. It may, for example be enough for an entity to *resemble* a bicycle in order for us to label it a 'bicycle'.

Do you think that the other arguments for God deserve to go extinct? For example, according to the cosmological argument, there must be a timeless, spaceless, personal cause of the universe. When we're asking questions about the origin of the universe, are we getting any closer to a meaningful discussion?

Yes, I think the cosmological argument gets us closer to a legitimate discussion. I would say it's an argument that I would like to see evolve rather than go extinct. For example, the discussion is particularly interesting when we're exploring questions relating to the Big Bang. The Big Bang opens up lots of questions about the nature of time, such as what we mean when we say that something existed 'before' the start of time. Does 'time' have any meaning in this context? That's a good question to ask.

What we can say with confidence, however, is that introducing God to solve this problem gets us nowhere. Without evidence of God's interactions with the world, how can we test whether God was responsible for the Big Bang? How could a being without a physical body interact with a world that is made up of physical matter? Any answers to these questions will be pure speculation. The cosmological argument is based upon the intuition that an agent must be responsible for things that we don't understand; in my opinion,

God doesn't appear any more likely than plenty of other wild guesses. If there is a necessary being, then let it be the universe.

Another popular argument for God's existence is the design argument. The world, says the theist, is so complex that it is far more likely to be the product of design than the result of chance. Do you have any sympathy for this argument?

None at all. Before Darwin's dangerous idea, philosophers and theologians held quite a naïve, <u>anthropomorphic</u> understanding of God. The idea was that because the world appears to be full of complex environments and well-adapted creatures, God must be some kind of handyman: a flawlessly clever person who designed and created the world for the enjoyment of human beings. Darwin changed all of that. Now we know that

> If something is <u>anthropomorphic</u>, then it is a non-human entity that has been attributed (rightly or wrongly) human qualities. Describing jellyfish as 'malicious' is an example of anthropomorphizing.

the world was not deliberately designed by an intelligent designer but was the product of the long, blind process that is evolution by natural selection.

Interestingly, Plantinga once challenged me to a debate which we had in Chicago about natural selection and God; I took his arguments and turned them into *reductios*. That did involve a little bit of satire, but I think it was exactly called for. Plantinga, like many theists, argued that evolutionary theory was perfectly consistent with the idea of a creative god playing a role in it, and I thought: that's true! It's also true that that same theory is consistent with the idea that Superman's father guided the evolutionary process in order for Superman to have suitable playmates in the twentieth century. In fact, there's rather more evidence for my theory than for his! Plantinga disagreed:

> The Latin phrase '*reductio ad absurdum*' means 'reduction to absurdity'. All *reductios* (the short plural) aim to show that something has gone wrong with an argument's structure or premises. They do so by claiming that an argument's conclusion leads to absurd consequences.

'nobody could live for millions of years and fly faster than the speed of light', he told me. Come on! But somebody could walk on water?

Moving away from biology, theologians have turned their attention to physics. These days, religious philosophers will appeal to laws of nature that appear to be finely tuned, they say, to allow for the existence of intelligent life.

According to the theist, these laws of nature are so delicately balanced that they cannot be explained by chance alone. This argument doesn't stand to reason. The laws of physics can be explained in terms of physical chance and accidents. There's no need to introduce supernatural fine-tuners.

Do you think that the average believer is concerned with these kinds of arguments?

I think there are roughly three flavours of believers. For a start there are those for whom their religion just doesn't matter. These are the 'ignostics': they just ignore the whole thing. They don't care about faith or arguments for God; they're like people with a tin ear for music. They don't identify themselves as theists, atheists or even agnostics, they're nothing; they just get on with their lives. Then we have those who are interested in their religion. Here, there is a great chasm between two more types of believers: those who intellectualize religion and those who live by it. The latter are the people who follow the commandments of God and don't worry too much about whether the rules of their religion make sense. On the other hand, those that intellectualize religion recognize its problems and devote tremendous time and cleverness trying to resolve the tensions between what their tradition tells them and what they know from other sources. Religious intellectuals are a very devoted and intelligent group of people, yet they make almost no progress and the preachers of the world pay almost no attention to them.

The talking tree

Earlier on in our discussion, you suggested that we might be able to offer 'naturalistic' accounts for why people believe in God. Do you have any thoughts on what such an account would look like?

I have quite the tale to tell about the origin of religion. It's a 'just-so' story, but it has many testable elements that could prove to be true. It's a story about how our minds understand other minds, and it goes like this. When mammals and other vertebrates enter the world, they are born with an orientation response to anything sudden. Anything striking or unexpected, like a vibration or a sound, can set it off. For example, when your dog

> A 'just-so' story is a narrative or explanation that is somewhat speculative. In other words, it's a story that has not yet been verified. Most *confirmed* evolutionary explanations began as just-so stories.

hears a thump outside of the window, they become alarmed and start to bark. This response leads the dog to start scanning the environment. Now, what is it that your dog is looking for? Well, they're not looking for *what* is there, but *who* is there. The cause of the noise was probably harmless – snow falling off the roof perhaps – but evolution has taught the dog that it's better to be safe than sorry.

Humans have this same agent-detection system. Let's consider another example. I want you to imagine that two of our ancient ancestors are searching for fruit on a dark, windy night in the woods. Foraging for some berries, suppose that one of our gatherers hears a whistling sound just out of sight. This whistling sets off their 'who was that?' alarm. They can't just let it go; it can't just be the wind. 'Better safe than sorry', says evolution. So, persistent doubts creep in until they've convinced themselves that there's another agent in the woods. One of the foragers asks the other, 'Did that tree just speak?', and that really sparks their imagination. Leaving the forest, our ancestors discuss the talking tree on their way back to their village, and then they share their story with anyone who will listen. By the next day, everybody in the village is gossiping about the talking tree. At first, a lot of the villagers aren't going to believe in it, but the kids are going to believe in it, and the next time someone is out in the woods at night, they'll be primed to believe it too.

If this type of behaviour is happening in most human communities, it won't be long before every village has its own menagerie of goblins, ghosts and gods. Over time, the most interesting and exciting deities will survive as their stories will be passed down the generations, but the boring ones will die out. In the end, an established group of gods – that might all serve particular purposes – will be all that's left. This is what we call 'polytheism'. Polytheism evolves into monotheism when religion finds itself in conditions where having an ultimate authority is vitally important. Think about how useful it would be if there were one single source of power that everyone can agree to obey. If people behave themselves, they'll be rewarded with infinite happiness in heaven; if they neglect their duties, they'll be punished for eternity in hell. It wasn't long before kings, priests and tribal leaders understood this.

Do you think that these leaders adopted religion for political purposes, or did they genuinely believe what they were preaching?

I think it's plausible that they had faith in what they preached. Typically, however, ideas only survive the test of time if they serve a purpose. The success and order that monotheism established would have encouraged future leaders to continue the tradition of their ancestors. If it didn't benefit them, then it probably wouldn't have survived.

At the same time, it seems that religion also serves to benefit society. After all, places of worship are often used to foster community and offer help to those in need. Do you think that religion is also a force for good?

Well, I think that's about right. Some forms of religion are a great thing. There is a wonderful poem by Robert Frost that sums up my thoughts on the matter. Frost captures it quite nicely when he says, 'Home is the place where, when you have to go there, they have to take you in.'[2] Religious institutions from all cultures offer to be that home, to anybody who needs a place to belong. This is something that the state does not provide, and I think it's wonderful that religion takes on this role. With that said, it's important that we separate the good deeds of the religious from their histories and metaphysics. I have great respect for the more evolved forms of religion that are becoming more secular and reducing their creed to the straightforward message of helping those in need. My hope, and expectation, is that all religions will eventually give up on their supernatural speculations and embrace the world that is left behind.

My fellow horseman, Richard Dawkins, would like to see religion go extinct. I like to tease him about this. I say, 'Richard, you should take a more evolutionary approach.' He should recognize that dinosaurs didn't go extinct, their descendants are flying in every tree, and they're wonderful; they're delightful! What we really want to do is encourage religions to evolve into socially benign communities and organizations, which some of them have done. If those were the only religions around, there would be no problem. So, I don't agree with Christopher Hitchens that religion poisons everything – but it comes close – and I think that those who want to defend religion have a very tall order in publicly disassociating themselves from the excesses in their own religious traditions. This is not easy: it can even be very dangerous to do. However, we should encourage it, and we should do what we can to avoid the set of attitudes which, right now, play into the hands of the fanatics in every religion.

Could you say more on this? What do you make of religion's existing legacy?

I think that theism used to be, and still is in places, a force for darkness and regression. Throughout the history of religion, the 'correct' picture of the world was handed down through elders and their traditions. Anything that threatened this tradition had to be ignored or suppressed, no matter how true it was. Many of the early scientists found this out the hard way. Fortunately, religion has made significant progress since the Reformation and now, in the modern era, it's changing at a rate that we have never seen before.

> In the sixteenth century, a movement of theologians sought to break away from the traditions of the Catholic Church. This movement was known as the 'Reformation'. The Reformation marked the birth of Protestantism, which rejected the Pope's authority and sought to make Christianity more accessible to ordinary people.

Religion has changed more in the past one hundred years than it has in the past thousand, and I think it will change more in the next ten years than it's changed in the last hundred. This is because religions are being forced to operate in a transparent medium that used to be murky. The epistemological fog that made it hard to know what was going on has disappeared. This is true of most institutions, such as universities and corporations, who have to change in order to deal with the fact that everybody's living in a glass house. It's the electronic era that's caused this change. Religion has thrived, to an extent, because it was able to keep secrets, but it's a lot harder to keep secrets these days. Before the internet, the Church was able to control the message it wanted to put out. In particular, they could dictate their own histories and keep their followers from learning about different worldviews. The digital age is changing everything; it takes about twenty years to grow a Christian, but only twenty minutes to lose one. Like every other institution, religion is going to have to catch up or it's going to become extinct.

From the perspective of the Church, it doesn't look like they're changing fast enough. The latest data is quite bleak. The Southern Baptists are baptizing about 300,000 people a year.[3] That's about the same as it was back in the 1950s, but here's the thing: back then, the population of the United States was half of what it is now. This is supposed to be the most 'thriving' mainstream religion in America. These numbers are significant because this is a Church that actively tries to get new converts. They want to retain their influence, but they're watching it slip away. Their numbers are plummeting. If you look at the age distribution of belief, the same thing is happening all over the world. Today's youth are giving up on the religion of their parents and embracing a secular worldview. If this continues, I think that religion as we know it will disappear, and the world will be a better place for it.

Evil, suffering and pessimism

It's curious that you haven't mentioned the problem of evil, which is probably the most popular argument against the existence of God. What do you make of the problem of evil?

Well, I appreciate the problem of evil because it forces theologians to perform all sorts of embarrassing mental gymnastics. Theologians spend their time trying to explain why their all-loving God would allow His creations to suffer and, each time they do, they slowly chip away at what little credibility they have. At this point, it should be obvious that there isn't a respectable answer to the problem of evil. Yet, they continue to look for clever ways of showing that they were right all along. Each time the theist gives a response it only proves to show that nothing an atheist could ever say would be able to change their mind.

Yujin Nagasawa has claimed that evil isn't just a problem for theists, but atheists as well. The unresolved tension, he says, is that atheists believe that evolution involves a tremendous amount of pain and suffering, however, atheists also think that the world is a good place, in which we should be grateful to live. How would you respond to the charge that atheism is hypocritical?

If Nagasawa is saying that natural processes are 'evil', then he doesn't understand what natural processes are. Many animals die prematurely: they get hit by lightning, they fall off cliffs, they get eaten by predators. Evolution ensures that those who are well-adapted pass on their genes and that those who are unfit die out without offspring. The lion eats the gazelle and the gazelle experiences pain and fear, there's no doubt about that. Yet, the lion is just eating. There are no morals here. The natural world – the pre-social world – is amoral. There is no 'good' or 'evil' when it comes to nature. I think we want to understand how our system of rules, taboos and norms come about. In my view, it all goes back to Thomas Hobbes.[4] Hobbes believed that before human society, there was no right or wrong. In other words, he thought that morality was a human artefact. That

> Thomas Hobbes (1588–1679) is one of the most important political philosophers in history. Hobbes believed that society was built on the principle of cooperation for mutual benefit. In a state of nature – a state without laws and law enforcement – 'the life of man', said Hobbes, would be 'solitary, poor, nasty, brutish, and short'. For Hobbes, the origin of morality coincides with the origin of the state. In his own words, right and wrong are 'qualities that relate to men in society, not in solitude'.

doesn't mean that it isn't real or important: it is the very basis for living in a free society. If morality is a human, social construct, then there is no morality when it comes to nature. To say that nature is 'evil' is to miss the point of morality.

So you do not believe that 'suffering' is <u>intrinisically</u> bad?

I reject the word 'intrinsic'. Almost never does the word 'intrinsic' do anything but serve as an excuse for not thinking hard enough. Intrinsic awfulness, like the intrinsic value of philosophy or the intrinsic nature of consciousness, are just cop-outs. I don't let people hide behind these phrases.

Let's think about why suffering matters. Every human being on the planet is the result of 3.5 billion years of incredible engineering. The consequence of this engineering – that is, evolution and education – is that every human being is a unique locus of projects, ideals, attitudes, hopes and fears tied into a network. That makes human beings a very special kind of thing. Suffering is the thwarting of such an individual's goals – a thwarting of one's projects, ideals and hopes – and the more complex and far-reaching the goals you have, the more suffering you're capable of. I don't think that oysters suffer. They have small hearts and organs, but they don't have a complex central nervous system. If you want to call that a capacity to suffer, then give me a good reason. In the case of human beings, however, we find all kinds of suffering – pain, torture, humiliation – which obtrude into our lives and make it impossible for us to live the way we'd like to. Letting people be themselves is about as high a value as you can have, except when their being themselves is going to hurt others. That's the point where morality should kick in: when one person causes another person to suffer, despite promising not to do so. Suffering is only 'bad' in the moral sense because it breaches the social contract.

> An action or entity is 'instrumentally' bad if it is bad for some further reason. For example, 'moving to Paris' is bad *because* everybody in Paris is unhappy. In contrast, something is '<u>intrinsically</u>' bad if it is bad *in and of itself*. For example, some philosophers argue that 'being unhappy' is just bad. Ask yourself: does it make sense to ask a Parisian *why* they don't want to be unhappy?

What do you think of these more general statements about the world's overall value, such as the claim that the world contains 'more good than evil'?

I think that quantifying these things is hopeless. Whether it's the relief of escaping certain death at the hands of a predator or the rags to riches story of somebody overcoming the obstacles of poverty, so much of the good in the world arises from escaping evil. I think the very idea that you can put the good on one side and the evil on the other and weigh them up is ridiculous. Life isn't chess. In chess, you can determine a good or bad move because each decision helps achieve a victory, draw or loss. After the game, the players can review every choice without ambiguity; we can see, objectively, whether some move was good or bad. In life, however, we never get that perspective, and we never will. Whether the world is 'better' with some good or evil is beyond our ability to say. So, I don't think anyone can say whether or not the world contains more good than evil. What I would say, however, is that humanity has made tremendous progress on this front. Life is better than it ever used to be for many people alive today. I'm in absolute agreement with Steven Pinker about this.

> Steven Pinker is a popular cognitive psychologist. In his books *The Better Angels of Our Nature* (2011) and *Enlightenment Now* (2018), Pinker argues that people – throughout history and across the world – continue to live longer, safer, healthier and happier lives than their predecessors.

Pinker has done a great service in showing us how much better the world is now compared to the world of our ancestors.

Despite all of the pain and suffering, do you think that this is a world we should be grateful to live in?

In the context of evolution, you see how everything alive today is in one sense profoundly lucky, not unlucky, to be alive. Ninety-nine per cent of everything that has ever lived has died childless, but not a single one of our ancestors did. That's true of every fox, every fly and every blade of grass. If that's not an object of wonder, I don't know what is.

On a personal level, I feel gratitude when I think about my life, and I think it's a shame that there's no suitable recipient for that appreciation aside from my fellow human beings. If there is a moral imperative, it's to try and make the world a better place. It's a way of honouring all the benefactors that you have had, going back thousands of years, who have done so much to improve our lives. One way we can improve the lives of others is to have proper religious education. It would be wonderful if everybody could receive compulsory education about the religions of the world. I've always been a proponent of this. If we can educate the world's children to the other alternatives, then this will have a profound effect on who takes religion seriously and why.

Afterthoughts

The new atheists aren't just appreciated for their ideas, but the way in which they communicate them. Of course, this interview captures many of Dennett's thoughts on philosophy of religion, but – no less importantly – it illustrates why people love the four horsemen: they're honest, direct and never pull their punches. Dennett wastes no time in exorcizing what he sees as supernatural, outdated concepts; there are no essences, no senses of the divine and no mind-independent morals. It's time that religious philosophers grew up, he says, and got on with something worthwhile. Instead of defending fantasies, they should figure out where religion came from and where (or whether) it should go.

The question of how religion will change is a fascinating one. Dennett's claim that the trend of history is that of increasing secularization seems correct. While some people may always believe that priests have the power to transform bread and wine into God's body and blood, or that Muhammad flew to heaven on a winged horse, whenever the principles of the Enlightenment manage to take hold, beliefs in the supernatural become weaker or lose their grip entirely. How far this will go is too difficult to say. Even if the natural sciences could explain the world's origin, laws of nature and moral values, I doubt that humans will ever shake the feeling

> The Age of Enlightenment (seventeenth–eighteenth century) was a European intellectual movement. The 'ideals' of the Enlightenment include science, reason and a non-supernatural approach to ethics and meaning.

that 'there's *more to life* than this'. We all know somebody who describes themselves as 'spiritual but not religious'. 'I think there's something else out there', they say, 'and it's probably not Apollo, Allāh or Superman. But I believe there is *some* reason why we're here.' All of the science in the world couldn't break that spell.

Questions to consider

1. Does Reformed epistemology lead to absurd consequences?
2. How plausible is Dennett's just-so story about the origin of religious belief?
3. To what extent are essences outdated concepts?
4. Is the pre-social world an amoral world?
5. Do you think that religion will change for the better?

Recommended reading

Advanced

Daniel Dennett, *Breaking the Spell: Religion as a Natural Phenomenon* (New York: Viking, 2006).

> If you enjoyed this chapter, then this book is a must-read. The 'spell' which needs breaking, says Dennett, is that religion closes itself off from scientific investigation. Uncovering the origins of religious belief, Dennett explains how religion will evolve, how it should be taught and whether it leads to a more fulfilling life.

Alvin Plantinga, 'Reason and Belief in God', in *Faith and Rationality: Reason and Belief in God*, ed. Nicholas Wolterstorff and Alvin Plantinga (Notre Dame, IN: University of Notre Dame Press, 1983), 16–93.

> Here, Plantinga gives his account of one the most important developments in contemporary philosophy of religion: Reformed epistemology. Plantinga claims that belief in God is justified in the same way as belief in the external world – that is, it is a 'basic belief' that is grounded in sensory experience. You do not need arguments or proof to justify your belief in the external world; by the same token, says Plantinga, you do not need arguments or proof to justify your belief in God.

Intermediate

Daniel Dennett, *Darwin's Dangerous Idea: Evolution and the Meanings of Life* (New York: Simon and Schuster, 1995).

> Merging philosophy and science, Dennett makes a case for Darwinian evolution as an undesigned, blind process that can account for the existence of intelligent life. In Chapters Sixteen and Seventeen, Dennett explores the question of how morality can be grounded in nature.

Daniel Dennett and Alvin Plantinga, *Science and Religion: Are They Compatible?* (New York: Oxford University Press, 2011).

> In 2009, Daniel Dennett and Alvin Plantinga took part in a debate in which they discussed whether theism is compatible with (or required in the light of) the discoveries of physical science. The book includes a transcript of the original debate – in which Dennett rejects Plantinga's assertion that evolutionary theory requires an intelligent designer and compares Christianity to Supermanism – as well as a series of original replies.

Beginner

Daniel Dennett, 'Show Me the Science', *New York Times*, August 2005, www.nytimes.com/2005/08/28/opinion/show-me-the-science.html.

> In this concise and witty piece, Dennett rails against the view that intelligent design should be taught in high schools. Intelligent design, which maintains that the complexities of life exceed the explanatory power of evolutionary theory, posits the existence of a supernatural designer. Dennett suggests that intelligent design might be 'one of the most ingenious hoaxes in the history of science' and says that students, if studying it at all, would benefit from tracing the origin and success of such frauds.

Richard Dawkins, Daniel Dennett, Sam Harris and Christopher Hitchens, *The Four Horsemen: The Discussion That Sparked An Atheist Revolution* (Penguin Books: New York, 2019).

> In 2007, four thinkers – who would become the 'four horsemen of new atheism' – recorded a conversation that inspired a new wave of interest in atheistic philosophy. Once their two-hour, unmoderated, cocktail-fuelled discussion had gone viral, the horsemen's thoughts on the metaphysics, ethics and cultural impact of religion had defined a generation. This book – which includes accompanying essays from Dawkins, Dennett and Harris, as well as an introduction by Stephen Fry – is the transcript of that infamous conversation.

Chapter Ten

The Rationality of Theism

Silvia Jonas

Introduction

The more we know, the less we need God. As philosophy strides forward, superstition stumbles back and, eventually, questions of theology are replaced with questions of science. As we have seen, this is the spirit of the new atheist's frustration with the God of the gaps: 'The Deity of Craig and Swinburne', they say, 'lingers in the cracks of scientific knowledge.' It's no wonder that as science progresses, and the smaller these cracks become, the less air theism has to breathe.

Our guide for this chapter is one of philosophy's most innovative and insightful big-picture thinkers, Professor Silvia Jonas. Jonas has made invaluable contributions to a range of topics, including – but not limited to – the philosophy of science, logic, mathematics and, of course, religion. Silvia's views aren't bound to either side of the debate. Instead, her approach calls for a new era of discourse that recognizes the virtues of scientific inquiry, while being unrestrained by the vices of one-sided thinking.

According to Jonas, the new atheists are justified in their frustration: it's unreasonable for theism to think it can compete with physics or biology. However, that doesn't mean questions of God aren't important. The empiricism of the Enlightenment may have taken hold, but we still find meaningful discourse in abstract, non-tangible concepts such as morality, modality and mathematics. So, why should questions of God be treated any differently? Rather than kicking God off the stage, perhaps God just needs recasting. Maybe then, thinks Jonas, God will find an audience that doesn't see theism in conflict with contemporary philosophy, but as a part of it.

Theism exits centre stage

In one form or another, questions about God have always played a key role in Western philosophical thought. In antiquity, Plato, Aristotle and Plotinus each argued for a particular view of God as initiating cause of the world. Medieval philosophy, reflecting Jewish, Christian and Islamic influences, was characterized by detailed theological discussions of God's attributes and provability. When the Scientific Revolution, which started in the sixteenth century, turned hitherto mysterious phenomena into predictable natural events – for example, through the groundbreaking discoveries of Kepler and Newton – this led to an emancipation of reason from religious faith and marked the beginning of 'modern' philosophy. Interestingly, however, there was still an explanatory role for God despite the rise of science – as the source of causality (Leibniz) or perception (Berkeley), as a regulative ideal (Kant) or as Absolute Spirit (Hegel). Even when, in the nineteenth century, philosophical thought turned distinctly hostile towards religion, discussions of God still took centre stage: religion was the 'opium for the people' (Marx),[1] a dead cultural force (Nietzsche) or a projection of the mind (Freud).

It was only with the rise of logical positivism in the 1920s that God was definitively banned from mainstream philosophical discourse. Logical positivists, like Otto Neurath and Rudolf Carnap, argued that statements are

---

Plotinus (*c.* 205–270) was the founder of Neoplatonism – although, he just called it 'Platonism'. The Neoplatonists thought that everything radiated from a single, divine unified state of absolute consciousness: the 'One'.

Nicolaus Copernicus (1473–1543) hypothesized that the Sun, and not the Earth, was at the centre of the universe. Developing Copernicus's view, the astronomer Johannes Kepler (1571–1630) made groundbreaking discoveries regarding the laws of planetary motion.

Immanuel Kant (1724–1804) was a key figure of the Enlightenment. Kant didn't think we could *know* that God exists; instead, Kant said that God was a prerequisite to a coherent moral philosophy. A just universe requires God to regulate it and, therefore, we ought to postulate God's existence.

According to Karl Marx (1818–1883), religion is 'the heart of a heartless world, and the soul of the soulless conditions'. In other words, people cling to the illusion of religion to escape their social and political troubles.

only factually meaningful – and thus, worth philosophical attention – if they are verifiable by empirical observation. Since, as is well-known, we can neither empirically observe nor logically prove the existence of God, logical positivists decided that statements about God are meaningless. Of course, the heydays of logical positivism are long gone, yet the rise of positivism and its influence marked the beginning of a number of developments due to which theism eventually lost its status as a worthy topic of philosophical inquiry. For

> The Vienna Circle was a group of prominent philosophers and scientists; they held regular meetings at the University of Vienna between 1924 and 1936. Towards the end of his life, one of the groups leading figures – A. J. Ayer (1910–1989) – said that 'nearly all' of the Circle's shared philosophy – logical positivism – turned out to be false.

example, it is now common sense to reject any form of dogmatic belief, such as belief in the literal truth of sacred religious texts or belief in traditional characterizations of God as omnipotent, omniscient and benevolent. Today, it is also widely known that religious faith, whether grounded in the actual existence of God or not, comes with evolutionary benefits that make it easy to explain scientifically why people end up having such beliefs. For example, it's easier to face death if you believe that an all-loving God is waiting for you in heaven, just as it's easier to bear the glaring injustice and cruelty of the world if you think it's all part of a divine plan. Thus, the thought goes, if we can give a scientific explanation of why people have religious convictions, then there's no need for supernatural explanations. Finally, given that the physical manifestation of theism is not only individual believers but religious institutions, it is plausible to assume that the philosophical disinterest in theism has been fuelled by the well-grounded scepticism that many people feel towards organized religion. Because of all this, today's philosophical mainstream has largely ceased to engage with questions about God at all.

Perhaps this sounds exaggerated. After all, some research is still conducted on questions concerning theism and religion. However, compared to the number of people publishing in other fields – epistemology, philosophy of science and ethics, for example – and the number of philosophers who had something to say about God in the last 2,000 years (pretty much all of them), today, philosophers of religion are a tiny minority. Moreover, while much of the work that is published in, say, philosophy of science, has implications for epistemology, metaphysics and philosophy of mind – think about questions concerning causal models – most published work by philosophers of religion is considered irrelevant to other fields. Alvin Plantinga, for instance, one of philosophy of religion's canonical figures, advises Christian philosophers not to let their philosophical work be 'circumscribed by what either the sceptic or the rest of the philosophical world thinks of theism' – dismissing the difference in pre-philosophic assumptions between theists and atheists as 'wholly irrelevant', and rejecting the very idea that theist and atheist

> In philosophy of science, causal models are used to track the values and probabilities of a system in order to predict its future behaviour. To take an example, causal models may be used by computer programmers and philosophers of mind to plan and predict machine learning.

philosophers are engaged in a 'common effort' to determine the 'plausibility of belief in God'.[2] Thus, a central feature of contemporary philosophy of religion is its isolation.

A new distribution of roles

Is it really true that questions about God, theism and religious faith have become as obsolete as their shadowy existence in contemporary philosophy might have us believe? What is indisputable is that theism is no longer a popular position in large parts of Europe, which identifies itself as 'enlightened'. Equally indisputable, however, is the fact that in other parts of the world religion continues to play a central role in people's lives and thought. Perhaps God, theism and faith no longer belong to the core topics of most Western philosophy faculties simply due to a historical development, one that's captured in the attitude: 'we are no longer religious ourselves, so we don't need to understand religion'?

Things are probably not quite that simple. To understand why questions about God are not obsolete, first we need to clarify what exactly we are rejecting when we reject theism. The eminent philosophers of religion Richard Swinburne and William Lane Craig, for example, understand theism as a hypothesis that explains why the world is the way it is. Yet, if theism is indeed to be understood as an 'explanatory hypothesis', then it's not difficult to see why it has so few adherents in the modern world. Not only do the natural sciences provide much more convincing explanations for empirical phenomena, but they can also make accurate predictions about them. In this context, John Cottingham calls upon 'Einsteinian relativity, quantum mechanics, and the elegant mathematical theory called "inflation" to account for the unfolding of the universe'. Then, he says, 'Add to that the success of the Darwinian model of evolution by random mutation and natural selection . . . and we have an extraordinarily rich explanatory structure worked out in the crucible of a rigorously constrained methodology, and meticulously tested against a formidable body of observational evidence.'[3]

> John Cottingham is a prolific Christian philosopher. In his essay, 'Transcending Science' (2018), Cottingham defends atheism's irritation with God being treated as an 'alternative explanatory hypothesis'.

Measured against the natural sciences, theism has comparatively little to tell us about what holds the world together at its innermost folds. And in reliably predicting the future, theism is an utter failure.

One might object that the natural sciences leave many fundamental questions unanswered – they cannot, for example, explain why anything exists at all, what awaits us after death or why the universe is fine-tuned for life. So, it might, at first sight, seem natural to bring in God when the sciences can't answer a pressing question. For example, one might argue that the reason anything exists at all is because God wished for something to exist. Similarly, one might argue that the theory of evolution cannot explain irreducible complexity. If there are irreducibly complex natural phenomena, such an argument could go, then the theory of evolution would not be able to explain it, so we should assume that the complexity is due to God's intelligent design.[4]

There are two problems with this argument. The first problem is that nobody can guess what science will be able to explain in the future. Who knows if science will answer the question of whether there's life after death? Second, if we're only introducing God as an explanation when we don't have a scientific one, then theism will always have its back against the wall. As Dietrich Bonhoeffer points out, 'If in fact the frontiers of knowledge are being pushed further and further back (and that is bound to be the case), then God is being pushed back with them, and is therefore continually in retreat. We are to find God in what we know, not in what we don't know.'[5, 6]

> Dietrich Bonhoeffer (1906–1945) is celebrated as a theologian and role model. Bonhoeffer called upon Christians to rid themselves of 'cheap grace' – that all God requires is belief and church attendance. Instead, he thought Christians should commit to 'costly grace' – to follow Jesus's example and submit their lives to God's will. Bonhoeffer was executed by the Nazi regime for conspiring against Hitler.

Interpreting theism as an explanatory hypothesis, that can compete with the natural sciences at its gaps, has become an obsolete way of thinking. This, however, does not mean that theism itself has become an obsolete topic. In fact, there are many open questions about God awaiting philosophical investigation.

Theism re-enters centre stage

Let's go back to what we know as fact. Undoubtably, the vast majority of people across the world hold on to some version of theism. There are somewhere between 450 and 500 million non-believers worldwide; that's roughly seven per cent of the global population.[7] People identifying as theists come from a variety of educational backgrounds. While it is true that atheism is common among those benefiting from higher education, it is also true that, in some cases, those with higher educational attainment fall below the national average for atheism – South Korea and Germany are good examples of this.[8] Believing that theism is a mark of the uneducated is simply unjustified. Treating theism as a mere psychological phenomenon also falls short of the mark; such explanations fail to account for theism's complexity. For example, some studies suggest that religious belief satisfies a human need for meaning, group cohesion and collaboration, and helps us deal with existential fears such as death.[9] This makes perfect sense and, as such, offers one dimension of an explanation of why people end up having religious beliefs. However, explanations pertaining to the psychological benefits of religion are always going to be missing something. For example, they don't explain why some people hold on to their beliefs even if they are the source of anxiety or suffering (imagine a believer who is deeply afraid of purgatory or one who cannot understand why an all-loving God would allow for so much evil). Moreover, it's not clear how, exactly, explanations from evolutionary psychology are supposed to undermine religious belief. Typically, a belief is undermined if we can show that the mechanisms involved in the formation of that belief were unreliable – as is the case, for example, when we form beliefs under the influence of hallucinogenic drugs.[10] It is not clear, *at all*, that the belief-forming mechanisms of evolution are unreliable in the same sense as hallucinations. Belief in God is widespread. It's a belief held by people of all educational backgrounds, which is not undermined by evolutionary psychology. Therefore, I see no good reason why philosophers should refrain from investigating theism.

There are many questions about God that can only be answered philosophically, given that they fall outside the scope of the natural sciences.

For example, is it possible to interpret theism in a way that satisfies the intuitions of religious believers, while not presenting theism in competition with the natural sciences? Is there a definition of God that matches this interpretation? What does it mean to hold an ontologically committed (that is, a realist) position with regard to such a God, and how can religious belief be understood against the background of such an alternative definition of theism?

It is worth keeping in mind that God-talk is not the only kind of talk that refers to non-standard entities. For example, most people believe that 'Torturing babies is wrong', that 'Donald Trump could be the next president of the United States' and that '2 + 2 = 4'. What is it, exactly, that makes these sentences true? Well, to take them in order, we have a moral fact, a modal fact and a mathematical fact. But what *are* such facts? Are they part of the physical world? Can scientists observe them in labs? Surely not. However, most people are committed – both in the way they talk and in the way they act – to the existence of such facts. When we discuss what's right or wrong, things that could happen in the future or problems in mathematics, we express propositions that extend beyond the empirical. Yet, we appeal to their objective validity. This is interesting because the questions metaethics, metaphysics and philosophy of mathematics ask about such propositions are structurally *identical* to questions in philosophy of religion. For example, they ask whether it's possible to justify a belief in the existence of non-spatiotemporal entities – a question that has been asked about God for centuries. They also ask whether scientific explanations of *why* people form moral, modal or mathematical beliefs are enough to make sense of the roles they play in our lives – again, analogous to questions that are discussed with

> By 'non-standard entities', Jonas is referring to entities like numbers, values or God, that cannot be perceived in the same way as 'ordinary' objects, like flowers or cats.

> A modal fact asserts or denies the possibility (or impossibility) of a proposition. Examples of modal facts include: 'it is *impossible* to dislike tar water', 'it is *necessarily* delicious' and '*if* you drink it, you *will* feel better'.

> The word 'metaethics' refers to the branch of philosophy that explores the nature of morality. Metaethics asks important questions, such as: how can we tell good from bad? Is charity *good* in the same way that tar water is *good*? Do moral properties exist and, if they do exist, then where are they?

regard to scientific explanations of religious belief. Another important issue is epistemic access. Assuming that moral, modal and mathematical facts exist, how do we gain knowledge of these facts, given that we can't see them, touch them or otherwise perceive them? This is another question with a long tradition in theological discourse – we don't perceive God, so how do we obtain notions of God? Furthermore, one of the most important philosophical questions is how we should deal with disagreement. Let's say that an epistemic peer disagrees with you about the truth of a moral assertion like, 'Torturing is never justified.' In such a case, you need to ask yourself how, if at all, you should modify your belief. Are fundamental disagreements between epistemic peers – about moral, modal or mathematical

> An epistemic peer is somebody who's just as knowledgeable, intelligent and reliable as you are. In this context, the person disagreeing with you possesses the same information and abilities: their brains are working, and they're not missing any information about babies, morality or torture.

assertions – enough to undermine the reality of these domains? Should I stop believing in the objective truth that 'torturing babies is wrong' because somebody else believes it's not true? These questions are legitimate questions to ask. Yet, God-talk isn't any different.

Many of the questions debated for centuries with respect to theism are still discussed in philosophical communities, but with regard to domains more compatible with the current Zeitgeist: morality, possibility and mathematics. This shows that our interest in the question of whether reality extends beyond the physical realm is unbroken. Once we admit this, however, it takes only a small step to see the relevance of theism. Instead of artificially excluding questions about God from philosophical discourse, both the new atheists and philosophy of religion should try to see metaphysics as a *holistic* enterprise, in which we ask similar questions about areas that not only matter to us on an abstract level, but shape our everyday behaviour. I believe it was from this holistic point of view that Bertrand Russell wrote the introductory words of his famous essay, 'Mysticism and Logic', which shall serve as my closing remarks.

> Metaphysics, or the attempt to conceive the world as a whole by means of thought, has been developed, from the first, by the union and conflict of two very different human impulses, the one urging men towards

mysticism, the other urging them towards science. Some men have achieved greatness through one of these impulses alone, others through the other alone. . . . But the greatest men who have been philosophers have felt the need both of science and of mysticism: the attempt to harmonize the two was what made their life, and what always must, for all its arduous uncertainty, make philosophy, to some minds, a greater thing than either science or religion.[11]

Afterthoughts

At the end of her piece, Jonas reveals the thread that ties her view together. The relevance of morality, modality and mathematics is indisputable. They are worthy objects of philosophical investigation, not because they fill some hole in our grand 'theory of everything', but because they shape our everyday lives. There is no reason, claims Jonas, why theism shouldn't be explored for this same reason. We see that the great Bertrand Russell echoed this sentiment: philosophy, unlike religion or science, can investigate the physical world *as well as* non-standard entities. Its ability to study and harmonize these two domains, he tells us, makes philosophy uniquely valuable.

This shouldn't be understated: Silvia's views are carefully balanced, but they're also radical. The idea that theism has a (modest) place in contemporary philosophy may be welcomed by some theists and atheists. However, I doubt that the philosophers representing these camps – at least, those we have encountered in this book – would be willing to accommodate the views of their rivals. Of course, that doesn't mean that we have to follow suit. Pulling ourselves away from the debate, we may be satisfied with such a view.

This view, however, will need some defending. After all, Silvia is taking issue with pretty much every philosopher in this book. On the one hand, she tells us that Swinburne and Craig are naïve to think that theism can compete with modern science. We must ask ourselves, 'How are we to refute the argument from fine-tuning and the *kalām* cosmological argument?' On the other hand, we'll need to tell the atheists – Blackmore, Dawkins, Law and Dennett – that evolutionary psychology tells us nothing about the rationality of theism. We're going to ruffle everyone's feathers.

Yet, there is still hope: there may be a hypothesis that can unite God and atheism. In search of this worldview, in our next chapter, we must journey East.

Questions to consider

1. To what extent should religious philosophers be concerned with atheism?
2. Why do you think philosophers are becoming less engaged with questions of God?
3. How might Richard Swinburne respond to Jonas's claim that God should not be treated as an explanatory hypothesis?
4. Can explanations from evolutionary psychology undermine religious beliefs?
5. Is talking about God different to talking about morality, modality or mathematics?

Recommended reading

<u>Advanced</u>

Silvia Jonas, 'Mathematical Indispensability and Arguments from Design', *Philosophia*, vol. 49 (2021): 2085–102.

> A (very) challenging academic paper in which Jonas discusses meta-natural hypotheses – such as mathematical realism and theism – and the credibility of using them as explanations for empirical facts. This paper is a great example of Jonas's thorough, big picture approach.

Silvia Jonas, *Ineffability and its Metaphysics: The Unspeakable in Art, Religion, and Philosophy* (London: Palgrave Macmillan, 2016).

> The focus here is separate from the topic of this chapter. Instead, Jonas asks whether there are disciplines – such as art, religion or philosophy – that can give us ineffable (indescribable) information. It's a lengthy and (very) tricky book, but there's a lot to be gained, especially if you're an experienced philosopher working in metaphysics or philosophy of language.

Intermediate

Renewing Philosophy of Religion: Exploratory Essays, ed. Paul Draper and J. L. Schellenberg (Oxford: Oxford University Press, 2017).

> This is a collection of short papers discussing the future of philosophy of religion. The essays from YujinNagasawa ('Global Philosophy of Religion and its Challenges') and Eric Steinhart ('Religion after Naturalism') come highly recommended – both of which are brilliant, broadminded reads for anybody working in the field.

New Models of Religious Understanding, ed. Fiona Ellis (Oxford: Oxford University Press, 2018).

> If you enjoyed this chapter and want to gain more perspective on the questions it raises, then this is the book for you. Here you'll find pieces from John Cottingham ('Transcending Science') and Silvia Jonas ('Modal Structuralism and Theism'), as well many other philosophers who think that theists ought to engage with an analytic philosophy of religion (and natural theology) more critically.

Beginner

Bob Harrison, 'On Being a Philosopher and a Christian', *Philosophy Now*, 1996, www.philosophynow.org/issues/16/On_being_a_philosopher_and_ a_Christian.

> If the arguments from our opening chapters aren't successful, then you might be left wondering how a professional philosopher could hold onto their belief in God. If they become exposed to the flaws of treating God as an explanatory hypothesis, then why don't they abandon their faith? In this short, personal reflection, Harrison explains why belief in God is not merely a matter of reason.

Tim Crane, *The Meaning of Belief: Religion from an Atheist's Point of View* (Cambridge, MA: Harvard University Press, 2017).

> The spirit of Crane's short and accessible book is similar to that of our concluding chapters: it hopes to close the gap between theism and atheism. What philosophers fail to recognize, says Crane, is that 'theism' doesn't refer to an outdated cosmology, but a worldview that places community – and our sense of divine purpose – at its centre.

Chapter Eleven

Ex Deo

Jessica Frazier

Introduction

So, here we are, at the forefront of life's greatest questions: where did we come from, and why are we here? The answers that we've encountered couldn't be more divided. Theism infuses the universe with meaning. We are born out of God's love and majesty, claims the theist, to which we shall return. As we have seen, however, God's alleged love is plagued by problems of evil and suffering. Atheism, on the other hand, replaces a self-existent God with a self-existent universe; we have overcome tremendous odds, declares the atheist, and now we are free to fashion the world, and its meaning, in our own image. Yet, if the universe – and all of its natural and moral laws – *began* to exist, then where did they come from? Neither position, it seems, holds all of the answers.

Our interviewee for this chapter is Jessica Frazier, expert in Hinduism and Lecturer in the Study of Religion at the University of Oxford. Owing to the success of her books, media appearances and the *Journal of Hindu Studies* – of which Jessica was a founding editor – Frazier's work is laying the foundations for a truly global philosophy.

Hinduism is billed as the oldest world religion. However, Frazier is keen to point out that its concerns are broader than just God; Hinduism is a rich and diverse tradition that touches on almost every aspect of philosophy. It's a philosophy that takes many forms, both theistic and atheistic, and the view that Frazier develops doesn't take sides. Instead, it bridges the gap between atheism and theism. There is no reason, Jessica argues, why God *and* the universe can't both be fundamental.

Journeying East

With over one billion devotees, Hinduism is the third-largest religion in the world. Yet, many people in the West seem to know very little about the tradition. Perhaps we should begin with what 'Hinduism' is?

Hinduism is not one particular doctrine but a mix of philosophies that came out of the Indian subcontinent. It contains a range of different views on almost everything, from language and logic, causation and consciousness, to ethics and fundamental reality. What most people know about Hinduism as a religion is that it has many gods and that it is broadly pantheistic. That's generally true; the classical tradition of Vedaānta emphasizes that there's one underlying fundamental reality – called '*brahman*' – and that the world and all of the gods are manifestations of that reality. That's an important foundation for the whole way that Hinduism thinks about the divine: it's universal, always present and the ultimate truth of everything we experience. However, that doesn't mean everyone thought it exists; atheists were accepted within Hindu culture, as well as atomists, materialists, panpsychists and so forth. Hinduism's three-thousand-year culture is no less diverse than European philosophy . . . and because there was no real concept of heresy, it was easier for everyone to explore new ideas.

> Traditional Hinduism is based on ancient texts called the 'Vedas'. These are treated as a timeless source of information about the universe and our place within it. While earlier parts of the Vedas focus on rituals, the later texts – the Upaniṣads – are more concerned with questions of philosophy. 'Vedaānta' – a word that literally means 'end of the Vedas' – refers to schools of thought which focus on the Upaniṣads.

> The word '*brahman*' denotes the essence of the cosmos and its self-sustaining origin.

If Hinduism is so diverse, how is it possible for us to speak meaningfully about it in simple terms?

Well, if I had to summarize its philosophical angle on life, I'd say that – where Buddhism focused on scepticism – Hinduism tended to focus on the most pervasive and fundamental features of reality. Hindu philosophers were pretty confident about the value of speculating on possible explanations for the world.

> Buddhism emerged in North India (fifth century BCE). Its founder, Siddhartha Gautama, rejected Hinduism's most important ideas – including *brahman* and the existence of the self (*ātman*).

So it's full of positive philosophical theories: atomists believed that reality can be explained as a kind of Lego built up of parts, the dualists believed that either forms or consciousness lie at the heart of all things and the <u>grammarian</u> philosophers said that reality is an infinite web of possible meanings. These Hindu views incorporated criticism but didn't stop there. They used them to develop a richer philosophy. Of course, it's hugely diverse . . . but that's the same as with any other tradition! Suppose that somebody asked you, 'Can we really talk about Western philosophy? After all, it contains so many opposed views!' Yet, Bertrand Russell and others were happy to speak of one tradition of '*Western Philosophy*'.

> The word '<u>grammarian</u>' refers to the study of grammar. A Grammarian philosopher explores the nature and meaning of language.

> In fact, this was the title of one of Bertrand Russell's best-known works, *A History of <u>Western Philosophy</u>* (1946).

That's really what philosophical traditions are: not a single position, but a conversation. It's the same for Indian, Chinese, African, Buddhist or any other major philosophical traditions.

Let's open our discussion of Hindu philosophy with the universe's origin. In the Vedas, we find a creation account that's a little confusing. In the beginning, it says, 'There was neither non-existence nor existence; there was neither the realm of space nor the sky beyond. What stirred? Where? In whose keeping? Was there water, a bottomless deep?'[1] This seems like a contradiction: how, before the world came into being, could there have been existence *and* non-existence?

Actually, the interesting thing is that it says we shouldn't think of reality 'before' the world as either existing (in the way we normally understand it) *or* not existing (like some dark empty space). It is a bit like asking what came before the Big Bang made space and time; anything we think of as being there or then is wrong, because there was really no 'there' or 'then'.

This text, 'the hymn of creation' (*Nāsadīya Sūkta*) is very ancient and it begins by asking what we can know about the beginning of the universe. It is a proto-philosophical text. When it asks whether there was a 'bottomless water', the hymn is referring to the ancient belief that the world emerged from a great empty sea. We find this same myth in the Hebrew Bible, Egyptian thought and ancient Greek philosophy. But this text questions that idea by asking what could the original stuff even be . . . is 'nothingness' even something that can exist? The *Nāsadīya Sūkta* questions the way that we understand whatever came before the time-space world. Plus religiously, it's quite subversive! By saying at the end that even the highest God in heaven couldn't know the start of it all – because it would 'exist' and so be part of the reality we're trying to understand – it questions whether any simple theism could be the answer. However, there must have been some source, since nothing can spontaneously arise from nothing. So, in its way, this three-thousand-year-old fragment points to the puzzle at the root of cosmology in physics, and ontology in philosophy: what is the root of the reality we experience?

On the one hand, Abrahamic faiths seem committed to the idea that God created the world *ex nihilo*. On the other, from what you're suggesting, Hinduism seems more open to the idea that the world was created *ex deo*. Is that a fair description?

I think that's right. The hymn of creation doesn't say that the world was created out of something – it just leaves the question open. Later, Hindu metaphysics says precisely that some fundamental reality must have *become* the world, rather than making it out of something else. The word Sanskrit uses is 'Srishti', which means 'flowing'. The ultimate ground of being *flows* into the cosmos. *Ex nihilo* isn't treated as an option. It seems absurd; what would it even mean to make something appear without any material, formal or efficient cause, out of *nothing*? Empirically, we have no precedent for that possibility. In some sense, it must have emerged from something and, if that ultimate reality was divine, then the world wasn't created *ex nihilo*, but *ex deo*.

> The Latin phrase '*ex nihilo*' translates to 'out of nothing'. In contrast, '*ex deo*' means 'out of God'.

This may sound radical, but even Aquinas was a little uncomfortable with the idea of *ex nihilo* creation. In Aquinas's model, when God creates the universe, He's not making a brand-new thing that's completely separate from Himself. For Aquinas, whatever God created remains ontologically dependent on God.[2] That's very similar to the Hindu view we're discussing. These philosophies aren't worlds apart.

The Upaniṣads contain many descriptions of *brahman*. For example, in one story, a boy is struggling to understand *brahman*, so, his father tells him to add salt to a glass of water. The boy is confused: why is his father ruining a perfectly good glass of water? Once the salt has dissolved, however, the father explains. The salt, like *brahman*, is always there, 'it is the finest essence that constitutes the self and this whole world'[3] – an invisible essence that imbues every aspect of existence. Would you say the father's view of *brahman* is pantheistic?

This wonderful story is from the *Chandogya Upaniṣad*, an ancient text that's full of images of the world being suffused with the divine reality. I recently walked through an old cemetery in Washington D. C. where I'm from and came upon a gravestone. The stone's inscription read, 'I was but a wave, and now I return to the ocean.' That's another one of the Upaniṣad's beautiful metaphors – although it also turns up in the last episode of the TV series *The Good Place*. In a way, that inscription is pantheistic in its literal meaning that 'all is God'. *Brahman* has a constantly regenerative root. The *Chandogya Upaniṣad* illustrates this belief through an analogy of a tree. There is more to a tree than meets the eye – it isn't just its leaves, branches and trunk. A tree has a root: it grows back when you cut it down. Hinduism implies that beneath the surface reality has an undepletingly generative nature. Self-existent, all-creating, all-sustaining, infinite: in a sense Hinduism leans towards the physicist and says, 'Isn't this reality . . . well, sort of divine?'

> The *Chandogya Upaniṣad* is primarily concerned with questions of creation and metaphysics. Composed sometime between the sixth and eighth centuries BCE, its volumes are known for their colourful stories and metaphors.

> Produced by NBC, *The Good Place* (2016–2020) is a fictional television series which focuses on morality and the afterlife. Philosophers are perplexed as to why fans defend the show's aesthetic merits beyond its first season.

There is a branch, excuse the pun, of 'mystic' Hinduism that claims we'll never understand *brahman*'s nature. How should we interpret this idea?

Certain branches of thought treat *brahman* as a causal power with incredibly diverse manifestations that go beyond our own knowledge – maybe even beyond our conceptual capacities. Imagine trying to talk about *everything* that exists simultaneously. Is it red or blue? Is it in the past or future? If it's all of these things, including apparently contradictory qualities, then *brahman* is going to be difficult to comprehend in its totality. Plus the aspects of the reality that ground the empirical world may not be comprehensible in terms of time, space and familiar causation. Stephen Hawking said that asking what was before the Big Bang 'is like asking what lies south of the south pole'.[4] It's like that. The terms that define our thinking preclude us from formulating a complete answer! However, that doesn't mean the best explanation isn't correct as far as it goes.

In addition to explaining how the universe exists, we require an explanation for *why* it exists. According to Western monotheisms, for

example, an all-loving God created the world to share the gift of existence with other creatures. Why does *brahman* create the world?

That's a good question. The answer has to be that there's some disposition – an *intrinsic nature* of reality – that expresses itself in these strange worlds of stars, space, thoughts and feelings. For the Vedāntic realists and the <u>Kashmiri idealists</u>, the core essence of reality must naturally have dynamic, creative, emergent powers that flow into our kind of reality.

> Alongside Vedānta, <u>Kashmiri</u> Śaivism is one of the predominant idealist schools of Indian thought.

> According to <u>idealists</u>, physical matter is illusory; everything in existence, they say, is constituted by consciousness.

I'm struggling to understand why the world would 'flow' into existence. What are 'dispositions' and how are they internal to *brahman*'s nature?

'Dispositions' are just what a thing is or does. For example, I have a disposition to travel and do philosophy. What I'm suggesting is that whatever emerges from *brahman* must be natural to *brahman*'s nature. There's a notion called '*satkarya*' in India, which means that all of the changes something can undergo must exist in potentiality within its source. On this model, *brahman* always contained the potential for all of the beings and qualities that, in time, it would eventually become. You and me, and the weather tomorrow, and the last acts of human civilization and beyond: all of it must be part of the nature of things. Ultimately, the ground of reality has to be intrinsically creative and inter-relational; otherwise, nothing would have come to be in the first place. For the sake of illustrating the point, fire is a useful metaphor. Fire is intrinsically dynamic and complex: so if the basis of reality is less like clay and more like fire, then it's naturally going to change, transform and illuminate. That's just what fire does!

Some philosophers, such as Richard Swinburne, believe that God offers the best explanation for the universe's finely tuned laws. Hinduism seems to have a similar concept, '*ṛta*'. Is this another one of *brahman*'s essential properties?

In a sense, Vedāntic Hinduism agrees with Swinburne. If order were not embedded in the nature of the world, then everything would be a mess.

India's medieval philosophers made this argument: if there weren't a foundation to things, then at one moment, you'd be a human, then you'd be an elephant, some daisies, the colour red and then the number six. Fortunately, that's not how things are; you can't doubt the coherence of the empirical world. I think this shows that the source has to contain a blueprint of the world's order. Whether that's ṛta or some other principle, the template must exist at the fundamental level of reality itself.

> Within Hinduism, the principle that guides the world's order is ṛta. Ṛta is often compared to the Chinese concept of Tao: the underlying principle of the universe that secures coherence and harmony.

The gods

Many Hindus believe in gods like Brahma, Vishnu, Shiva and the Goddess. What makes these deities different to the God of classical monotheism?

As in Western cultures, some Hindus see the divine as a personal reality with awareness, creativity and love. For them, when you visit a temple and look into the eyes of the deities, you're both revering a particular god and also connecting with the world's ultimate foundation. There's a fantastic story in the *Bhagavad Gītā* where Krishna – an incarnation of the divine – is teaching his friend Arjuna about the nature of reality.[5] Arjuna asks Krishna, 'Would you show me your true divine being? As the foundation of reality? The energy behind everything? Please?' and Krishna replies, 'Sure, no problem.' Krishna proceeds to reveal his inner nature in what's called the 'Vishva-rupa' or the 'all forms manifestation'. He shows Arjuna all worlds and beings,

> Brahma, not to be confused with *brahman*, is the creator of the universe. Brahma has four heads, from which – legend has it – came the four books of the Vedas.

> Vishnu is responsible for protecting and preserving the universe. Depicted with four arms and blue skin, Vishnu has been incarnated nine times, the most recent being Krishna (a wise man) and Siddhartha Gautama (the Buddha).

> Shiva's job is to destroy the universe in order for it to be recreated. As the master of balance and rhythm, he is also known as 'Lord of the Dance'. In fact, it is one of Shiva's dances – the Tandava – which is said to destroy the universe.

all the gods and all that ever has or will exist in every possible world *inside* himself. It's one of the world's great images of the sublime, but it's also terrifying and Arjuna begs him to stop. This often reminds me of the stories from Ancient Greek mythology. The Greek gods would take human lovers, and their lovers would say, 'Oh Zeus, show me your divine reality. It's going to be amazing!' Zeus would reply, 'Okay. But, for the record, I don't think this is a good idea . . .' and then, invariably, Zeus's lover sees his ultimate form and is promptly reduced to a pile of ashes. Similarly, when the Hindu gods and goddesses reveal their true nature, mortals are blown away – mentally at least. Only the strongest devotees and philosophers can truly comprehend this core reality.

> The goddesses of Hinduism are often referred to, and worshipped collectively as, the great Goddess.

> The *Bhagavad Gītā* is another one of Hinduism's (many) central texts. The *Gītā* takes the form of an epic poem, in which the prince Arjuna discusses the philosophy of ethics and the soul with his friend Krishna.

The goddesses have an important place within Indian philosophy. Compared to the Abrahamic monotheisms, do you think that Hinduism has a more progressive outlook on divine femininity?

It does, especially when the Hindu deities are compared to the bearded father figure of Western religious art. Some religions treat the divine as a patriarch, representing law and protection. Others, however, emphasize divine purity (Shiva), wisdom and arts (Sarasvati), blessing and humour (Ganesha) or beauty (Krishna). With goddesses, there's a tendency to assume that they are going to be these fluffy, nurturing mothers. But Hindu goddesses are incredibly diverse. They can be about intellectual life (Saraswati), spiritual passion (Radha) or endurance and strength (Kali). One of my favourite examples is Durga – she is both the strongest warrior of all the gods and a maternal protector. The first time I went walking alone through the Himalayan mountains, I was worried about whether it was safe to wander on my own. Then, I came across a shrine

Durga

to Durga, the queenly warrior goddess – with her flowing hair and red sari – riding a lion and fighting a demon . . . and all while also holding aloft the lotus of enlightenment. There was something so empowering about it. She's an absolute rockstar – a hero! I think that's a really exciting portrayal of the divine, and of women too.

To draw another comparison, Vishnu takes physical form – partly – in order to 'play' (*līlā*) and enjoy the pleasures of the material world. By contrast, Jesus's motivations are quite different; he comes to earth to die on a cross. Does this tell us something about how Hinduism sees the world and its value?

Hinduism is a philosophy that aims towards the ultimate improvement of the world, and, for that, you have to believe that the world is worth improving. There's no concept of original sin, so matter isn't inherently bad and bodies aren't depraved. It's really about *what you do with them*. Many texts say one of the biggest problems in the world is ignorance, because close-minded people focus only on their own desires. By contrast, enlightened people always use life as a chance to learn more, increase beauty, alleviate suffering and rise to a higher level of existence. So, in that sense, you might find Hinduism to be a more liberating worldview than some other religions that focus on evil, law and punishment.

It's worth comparing Hinduism with Buddhism too. Buddhism focuses on suffering as the great motivator of human existence; we can't escape this suffering unless we achieve enlightenment. Hinduism says, 'Sure, suffering is a problem, and we should help avoid it. However, sometimes we have good reasons to endure suffering.' Take love, for example. Love involves compromise, often sacrifice and eventually an inevitable parting at death. Yet, it's worth it because those negative things are transmuted into something higher. Buddhism has trouble making sense of that idea. Hinduism, however, has all kinds of reasons for why existence itself has value. Often the gods symbolize these reasons: Krishna represents the beauty of nature, art and love, Lakshmi represents flourishing, Shiva represents higher understanding and so on. Even the fierce goddess Kali – who seems frightening at first – symbolizes the important place that struggle, suffering and death can have within the journey of life. Hinduism recognizes the nature of higher goods beyond mere pleasure and happiness; it's really quite existentially insightful.

The cycle of life

In the *Bhagavad Gītā*, we're told that the self (*ātman*) 'is not born, nor is it ever mortal', for it is 'ancient, unborn, eternally existing' and 'does not die when the body perishes'.[6] Most people know that reincarnation involves transmigrating from one body to another – like putting on new clothes – but what exactly does this belief involve?

Belief in reincarnation isn't just a part of Hinduism: it plays a significant role in Buddhist and Jain thought as well. It's a belief that can be found all over Asia, and of course classical Greece believed in it too. On the Indo-European interpretation, each person has an immortal core that moves along and takes various forms, life by life. We should be careful not to glamorize this process. It is unlikely that you were Cleopatra or Columbus in a previous life. Reincarnation isn't much fun, and why would it be? You've got to be born again; learn to speak again; go through puberty again; fall in love; get heartbroken; be happy; get old; and die – again, and again, and again, and again. It gives you the chance to develop as a soul, but otherwise it's not something to get excited about . . . in fact, you might want to escape that process eventually.

> Jainism is another one of India's popular religions; it teaches that every living thing has its own soul. Jain culture is well-known for its emphasis on *ahimsa* (the principle of non-injury), which involves a vegetarian diet and abstinence from root vegetables.

There is a concept within Hinduism called '*mokṣa*', a point at which we're liberated from the cycle of rebirth and achieve union with *brahman*. Is *mokṣa* similar to Christian ideas of heaven and, if so, is *this* something to get excited about?

There are different approaches when it comes to *mokṣa* and heaven. When I was a kid, the grownups told me that I was going to heaven. So, I'd ask them, 'Great! What will I do there?' 'You'll have as much ice cream as you like!' I thought, 'Wait a second! Ice cream is good, but forever?' If you're doing fun things forever, then it stops being fun. That conception of heaven as infinite pleasure is very different to ideas of *mokṣa*. The beatific vision is closer to it: returning to the world's source, seeing with divine eyes and having a connection to God

> Within Christian theology, the beatific vision is a heavenly state in which we are free of all desires and join God in Her perfect happiness.

and everything via the creator. There are many different ideas of *mokṣa* in different Hindu schools, but it's important to emphasize that *mokṣa* isn't just 'a new eternal life on the same terms but better'. In classical Indian thought, it is not just pain that is the problem with life; the problem with life is its finitude. So, the goal is not just painlessness but a transformation into something higher, more infinite and the transcending of worldly limitations. That means giving up your old identity. The idea of 'flowing back into the divine source' means you'll never be the person you were before. Yet, for Hindus, that's alright: you've already had that for an infinite number of lifetimes, and eventually it's time for something else. *Mokṣa* involves a readiness to become something new.

Should Hindus *want* to escape the cycle of rebirth? I can't help but think it would be pretty great to be incarnated as Taylor Swift. Is reincarnation as unappealing as you're making out?

If you want to aim at being a Taylor Swift, then that's fine. Do it millions of times if you like. Then, maybe you'll discover something else you want to do. Perhaps you want to become a painter, a photographer or a paramedic. There isn't a moral requirement to go in a particular direction – though, it would be cruel and rather egotistical to become a thief, a sadist or a murderer. Classical Hinduism agrees that there is a hierarchy of goods, and once you've tried all the lower ones, you may start to look up the hierarchy of needs to see a higher set of intrinsic goods to aim for. Some goods may even be superior to being Taylor Swift, as nice as that could be for a particular lifetime. In a way, the belief in reincarnation means that different goals don't need to compete with each other. Each can be appreciated for its own limited value, but we can also step up the ladder towards what is higher: from a hedonist, to a hero, to a sage, to something divine . . .

The good life

You say there isn't a moral imperative, but it seems like there is? After all, for the Hindu, the universe is governed by *karma*. If you earn good *karma*, like Taylor Swift, your reincarnation will be positive.[7] However, if you earn bad *karma*, like Kanye West, your reincarnation will be negative.

An earlier version of this chapter included several humorous references to Taylor Swift's hit song, *Karma*. At the request of the publisher, these lyrics have been removed to avoid any bad blood with Republic Records.

But as a cosmological belief about reality, *karma* is more like a natural law than an imperative. An imperative suggests an imperator, a lawgiver who will punish you if you don't do the right thing. For Hindus, there isn't a judgemental God studying your every move. Nobody's chalking up your actions to determine whether you've been naughty or nice. *Karma* is just a principle of nature and – to run with your popstar analogy – it acts automatically on Kanye, Taylor and the rest of us. You might end up creating bad *karma*, and you might even need to. After all, you might deem some purpose so important that you're willing to take the bad *karma* on board and put your spiritual journey back a few thousand lives. That's okay, you might even learn more that way, and it's not a moral issue since no one's going to suffer but yourself.

If there's no imperative to create good *karma*, does it make sense to describe actions as 'good' or 'bad'?

The West pretends that it's easy to say what it means for something to be 'good' or 'bad', and what they usually mean is 'compassion' versus 'cruelty' – being kind or vindictive. That's a very particular understanding of ethics, and it has nothing to do with most of the decisions that we make in our everyday lives. Think about the sorts of questions that you ask yourself: what should I do today? Should I paint a picture? Should I finish my essay? Should I tell my friend about a silly decision they've made? These questions are more complex than good versus bad.

Hindu ethics is primarily concerned with *dharma*: the proper functional order of things. There's a brilliant story of a tiger who comes across a holy man in a forest. The tiger thinks, 'Hey, look at him achieving liberation. I want to be calm and wise too!' So, the tiger sits down, takes the lotus position and meditates. Eventually, another wise man comes along and questions the tiger's decision. 'What are you doing? You're a tiger. It's actually pretty helpful for tigers to be tigers! If you don't be a tiger, the ecosystem's going to fall apart.' The tiger replies, 'Ah yes, I see; then I'd better be a good tiger!' And, of course, it promptly swallows the man whole. Being compassionate is an important aspect of any social situation, but Hinduism is wrestling with a more profound sense of the ethical: how we should live in the complex ecology of real-life situations. The *Bhagavad Gītā* talks about a similar concept called '*Loka-samgraha*', which means 'holding the world together'. If you want morality, then don't think about what's good or bad; think, 'What does this do for the world? Does it hold the world together?' Look at the big picture and apply your agency.

Philosophy of religion seems to be dominated by atheists and monotheists. The Abrahamic faiths defend themselves against the problem of evil, and atheists try to explain the world's nature without introducing God. Do you think that Hinduism can overcome this conflict?

It depends on the type of Hinduism you have in mind. If you think that *brahman* is an abstract reality, then you don't have to deal with the problem of evil or the problem of the unliftable stone. In other words, you don't have to deal with the problem that comes with treating God as a special kind of *person*. You can focus on the divine as the foundation of all existence, the principle that creatively drives all things and the transcendent reality within which the cosmos stands – from which it comes and to which it is going – and the deepest reality within our own human existence. Most of these ideas of the divine are quite different from what people like Richard Dawkins are rejecting – they're more compatible with what the West calls 'atheism', but they also bring out the vast power, beauty and eternal trajectory expressed in all things.

There are, however, plenty of Hindu theistic systems that believe in a personal God (or Goddess) and provide interesting philosophical arguments for this. How could time and space have begun, except by an initial non-caused cause that seems most like a case personal agency? What shaped the fundamental nature of things, and programmed in a coherent set of laws for the world such that it eventually produced Shakespeare? Rather like the cosmological and design arguments for God, these views say the world needs a pre-cosmic personal will in order to exist in the way it does. This idea of God stands separate from Abrahamic monotheism's theological ideas, so it doesn't necessarily commit to creation *ex nihilo*, divine judgement, heaven, incarnation or the image of a patriarchal God.

I suppose that's an important lesson to take. Hinduism has a lot to offer contemporary philosophy – in metaphysics, philosophy of mind, epistemology and ethics – and this is another example. A lot of debates in contemporary philosophy would benefit from Hinduism's insights; they just need to engage with it.

Afterthoughts

Despite being the third-largest global religion, scholarship in philosophy continues to ignore Hinduism's influence. Even in journals dedicated to 'international' philosophy of religion, academic papers on Hinduism rarely tally close to those focusing on the Western traditions. Frazier's work aims to overcome this disparity. As we have seen, Hinduism offers exciting new perspectives on metaphysics, morality, meaning and the self that European philosophy can only benefit from. It's about time that we brought these traditions into dialogue with one another.

There is an elegance to the orthodox Hindu metaphysics that shouldn't be overlooked. Unlike the dualism of classical theism, or the materialism associated with the new atheists, Hinduism places an ultimate core at the world's centre. Moreover, it may hold the keys to unlocking the problem of existence. The universe obviously exists, and it must have come from somewhere; so, why not infuse its origin with its existence? Moulding theism's self-existent God with atheism's self-existent universe, perhaps this ancient tradition can overcome our present-day tensions. Through philosophy, we may come to believe in *brahman*, and, through science, we may come to understand *brahman*'s nature.

At the same time, there are reasons to be sceptical of Hinduism's explanatory power. Guided by *karma*, classical Hinduism posits a cycle of rebirth that may generate more problems than it solves. At first, *karma* seems to explain the uneven distribution of worldly goods and evils, such as why some people possess fewer natural talents and wealth than others. Yet, because we can't remember our past lives, this system may seem arbitrary. If you bear no resemblance to the being that came before you, why should you suffer the consequences of their actions, especially when you can't even remember those actions? Frazier describes this process as non-moral; 'In the end,' she says, 'nobody will suffer but yourself.' Yet, somebody else *will* suffer: the person who replaces you upon your rebirth.

For Hindus, however, *karma* is just a fact of life: more of a natural law than an imperative. Yet, what evidence do we find of *karma* acting in the world? Is it any less reasonable to attribute triumphs and hardships to chance? If we don't have compelling reasons to think that *karma exists*, then perhaps we should suspend belief in it altogether. Otherwise, it is assuredly unfair, if not dangerous, to attribute people's misfortunes to their own misconduct. As Frazier points out, Hinduism is a diverse tradition, and some of its branches are more atheistic than they are supernatural. Therefore, there will be secular versions of pantheistic-Hindu thought that avoid these problems entirely. It is to these secular approaches to which we now turn our attention.

Questions to consider

1. In what way, if at all, are Hindu ideas of the divine preferable to Abrahamic monotheisms?
2. How can Vedāntic Hinduism respond to the *kalām* cosmological argument?
3. Do we have a responsibility to create good *karma*?
4. If reincarnation were true, would that make life less valuable?
5. Should we *want* to escape the cycle of rebirth?

Recommended reading

<u>Advanced</u>

Categorisation in Indian Philosophy: Thinking Inside the Box, ed. Jessica Frazier (London: Ashgate, 2014).

> A collection of academic papers that apply Indian thought to a range of philosophical questions, especially those concerning metaphysics and fundamental reality. If you enjoyed this chapter, then Frazier's entries – 'The Importance of Thinking Inside the Box', 'Metaphors for the Category of Existence' and 'The Order of Things' – are well worth a read.

Jessica Frazier, *Hindu Worldviews: Theories of Self, Ritual and Reality* (London: Bloomsbury, 2017).

> This is one of the best books on Hindu philosophy. The book is divided into three parts – matter, thought and practice – that illuminate Hindu ideas and apply them to central issues in modern philosophy. This book is perfect for professional philosophers or

graduate students looking to explore South Asian thought and gain
new perspectives in philosophy of religion.

Intermediate

Christopher Bartley, *An Introduction to Indian Philosophy: Hindu and Buddhist
Ideas from Original Sources*, 2nd edition (London: Bloomsbury, 2015).

> Bartley's guide to Hindu and Buddhist thought is absolutely
> outstanding. If you're a teacher or undergraduate looking
> for a comprehensive, far-reaching guide to the themes, central texts
> and insights of Indian philosophy, then this is the book for you.

Gavin Flood, *Hindu Monotheism* (Cambridge: Cambridge University Press,
2020).

> Exploring the philosophy and theology of Indian monotheism,
> Flood sheds light on how and why Hindus believe in an (infinitely
> expanding and contracting) supreme and transcendent deity.

Beginner

Kim Knott, *Hinduism: A Very Short Introduction*, 2nd edition (Oxford: Oxford
University Press, 2016).

> This is a first-rate introductory text. A concise and engaging
> overview, Knott covers all of the key areas, including Hinduism's
> history, scriptures, gods and festivals, as well as its relationship with
> contemporary issues such as class, gender and society.

Klaus K. Klostermaier, *Hinduism: A Short Introduction* (Oxford: Oneworld
Publications, 1999).

> It's hard to find an introduction to Hinduism that assumes no subject
> knowledge; somehow, this book manages it. If you're interested
> in learning about Hinduism as a philosophy and way of life, then
> this is the book for you. If you're more interested in the history of
> the tradition, then check out Klostermaier's other introduction –
> *Hinduism: A Short History*[8] – instead.

Chapter Twelve

The World Is God

Asha Lancaster-Thomas

Introduction

In the beginning, we were told that God – the omnipotent, omniscient, all-loving, timeless, spaceless Deity – created the universe. The atheists denied this. 'In the wake of modern science,' they said, 'we have no need for theism.' Some went as far as to claim that an 'all-loving' God wasn't just obsolete but one of the nastiest ideas we've ever had. Then, along came *brahman*. Hinduism offered hope; perhaps there's a supreme being whose nature is revealed to us through science, a being that doesn't fall victim to problems of evil, suffering and hell. And yet, the view that promised to unite God and atheism risked leaving everyone behind: multiple gods, an oscillating universe and an infinite cycle of *karmic* rebirth aren't easy pills to swallow. So, here, at the end of the road, we take our final shot at the great the mystery of existence.

Our final piece is from one of philosophy of religion's rising stars, Asha Lancaster-Thomas. In recent years, philosophers have become fascinated by alternative concepts of God. The literature surrounding pantheism, for example, has become a bustling marketplace of exchange, with pantheistic views being investigated, developed and critiqued more than ever before. It is here, in this marketplace, where we find Lancaster-Thomas.

Pantheism says that God is identical to the world: that God *is* the world. It's a view that isn't chained to souls, cyclical universes or realms of infinite happiness and suffering. If God is nothing more than the world, and science is studying God's nature, then perhaps pantheism can embody the spirit of atheism. Furthermore, according to Asha, this a worldview that can also offer us, here and now, meaning, morality and God. There is a catch, of course: there is no salvation. After all, how can we return to God if *we* ourselves are God?

God is everywhere

After you finish reading this sentence, I want you to close your eyes and reflect on everything you're experiencing – go on, it will be worth your while. Did you think about the air flowing in and out of your lungs? The soft sensation of cotton on your feet? The heat of the sun sneaking through the clouds? The sound of birds singing outside of your window? Now, what if I told you that *everything* you're experiencing is God? Perhaps you wouldn't find it so far-fetched. After all, many religions claim that God is everywhere. What I'm telling you, however, is that God is literally *identical* to everything that exists.

According to pantheism, when you reach out to pet your golden retriever, you're not just touching your dog . . . you're touching your God. In fact, your fingers, along with every other part of you, are components of God as well. Unlike the Abrahamic faiths – which understand God to be an immaterial, all-loving, all-knowing and all-powerful creator – pantheists are not tied to any of God's traditional attributes. Instead, pantheism puts forward the simple equation that 'God equals the world'. To be clear, the world isn't just our beautiful pale blue dot, but the entire cosmos. I'm not saying this to sell you on the idea that this chapter is divine or to outline the plot to another dreadful James Cameron movie. Rather, I want you to recognize that pantheism might be the best theory we have.

> Anaximander (*c.* 610–546 BCE) is considered to be one of philosophy's earliest pantheists. Anaximander sought to understand the origin (or '*archê*') of everything that exists. This origin, he believed, was the universe itself. Therefore, in virtue of the universe's immortality, he thought it to be divine.

The God particles

Many great pantheists have existed throughout history, from the Ancient Greek Anaximander and the Romantic poet William Wordsworth to the philosopher Baruch Spinoza.[1] After Spinoza brought pantheism into the spotlight, it grew in popularity well into the nineteenth century. (In fact, some scholars have gone as far as to say that Abraham Lincoln was a pantheist.)[2] In the past few decades, more and more philosophers have become interested in the idea that God is identical to the universe. They have been posing questions such as whether pantheism entails that God is fully physical, whether a pantheistic God counts as a person and whether the view amounts to anything more than just saying 'the universe exists'.

Let's delve a little deeper into what we mean by 'the world is God', a simple phrase that, as philosophers, we shouldn't take at face value. There are at least two ways of looking at it: that every *single* thing in the world is divine (distributive pantheism) or that the *whole* universe is divine (collective pantheism). I don't want to argue for either view here, but those are two of your options. Likewise, some pantheists see the physical world as the 'body' of God or as a physical representation, like an avatar. In contrast, others see the whole universe as the mind of God, with the world's creatures playing the part of neurons firing up God's consciousness. These are, I think, the most interesting questions: when we're talking about God, we want to know what God consists of.

There's a lot of debate as to whether William Wordsworth (1770–1850) was a pantheist or not. Yet, consider these lines from his poem, *A Few Miles above Tintern Abbey* (1798): 'And I have felt, A presence that disturbs me with the joy . . . Whose dwelling is the light of setting suns . . . A motion and a spirit, that impels All thinking things, all objects of all thought, and rolls through all things.'

During his time, the philosophy of Baruch Spinoza (1632–1677) was so controversial that he was banned from Jewish communities and branded a heretic. Spinoza's pantheism connects to his thoughts on the ontological argument, which – he maintained – showed that *at most* only one thing can exist. As we know that God exists, said Spinoza, everything that exists must be identical to God.

Abraham Lincoln (1809–1865) was the sixteenth president of the United States. As well as being the first US president with a full beard, 'Honest Abe' was the first president to be assassinated. During his life, Abe wasn't so honest about his religious views. Yet, after his assassination, his friends spoke of his 'elevated' pantheism and scepticism of the 'supernatural'.

The most common answer to what the world, or God, consists of is called 'physicalism'. According to physicalism, everything is made up of physical properties. In other words, *only* physical substances exist – things like books, air, light, density and mass. Philosophers are quick to remind us that matter, energy and space-time count as physical too – that is, anything that can be described by physics – even if we wouldn't usually call them 'physical'. Therefore, this view discounts the existence of non-physical entities like souls, spirits, ghosts and genies. However, the problem with this metaphysics is that

> An <u>avatar</u> is a figure who represents a person or god. There are exceptions, of course. For example, James Cameron's *Avatar: The Way of Water* (2022) represents the importance of thoughtful storytelling.

it struggles to explain consciousness. How do lots of physical properties give rise to (seemingly) non-physical consciousnesses? If God's going to make decisions, hear our prayers and contemplate our futures, then He needs to have thoughts.

Alternatively, the pantheist may claim that the universe consists of physical *and* non-physical properties. On this model, minds and brains can exist and interact in the same world. Although, how this happens is a mystery that even the dualists struggle with. How is it, exactly, that non-physical minds can interact with physical brains? This question has been asked for centuries, and it's unlikely that the dualists will have a solution anytime soon. Furthermore, it doesn't look like there are lots of non-physical minds interacting with the world; if there were, we'd expect all sorts of activity – little miracles – that couldn't be explained by physical science.[3] Yet, this is not what we find. Therefore, say proponents of idealism, you might think that the universe isn't physical at all: it's just one single spiritual being, an ocean of pure consciousness.

For idealists, only consciousness exists. There are no 'physical' properties. The universe is essentially one big, divine mind. This avoids the question of how souls interact with bodies and the problem of how consciousness arises in the universe. That seems like a more plausible view. However, you don't have to be an idealist to believe that the world is conscious; if any of the views I have mentioned is right, and can account for consciousness, then perhaps we can eat our cake and have it too. Suppose God is a conscious being who has agency; this will go some way in satisfying the theist who believes that God is a person. Likewise, if God is nothing more than the world before us, then maybe we can appease the atheists as well.

The kingdom of heaven

Imagine glimpsing a cascading waterfall in a deep, dark rainforest. Ponder the feeling of majesty you experience when you stand on the peak of a rugged mountain as the wind spirals around you. Have you ever put your eye to a telescope, encountered a cluster of stars in the Milky Way and felt overwhelmed by a sense of awe at the vast cosmos that engulfs you? Religious believers think that what you're experiencing is God's creation. However, according to pantheism, you are in awe of God itself. This God is quite different to the God of Abraham. So, what reasons do we have for thinking that Abraham was wrong?

One compelling motivation is the feeling I just described: a 'numinous' feeling. So many of us have felt this awe-inspiring, mysterious emotion well up inside of us when we're viewing a spectacular sunset or gazing at the moon over an obsidian ocean horizon. These experiences inspired Walt Whitman to write, 'I hear and behold God in every object.'[4,5] These experiences suggest that we're not just seeing awe-less entities, but divine ones. Equally, pantheism seems to account for the feeling of unity that we experience with other creatures and nature as a whole. Some scientists have proposed that the universe is driving towards connectedness, while others have endorsed the theory of eutierria. Many people feel something similar: as if they're part of something bigger, an interconnected whole that can be explained by the divine unity of pantheism.

> The word 'numinous' was coined by the philosopher Rudolf Otto (1869–1937). It refers to the feeling of being filled with the presence of divinity.

> The poet Walt Whitman (1819–1892) has been described as 'nearly' a 'pure pantheist'. 'Why should I wish', asked Whitman, 'to see God better than this day?'

> Think about how it feels to run through a forest, surf a gnarly wave or have your Marmite© sandwich stolen by a seagull. That's the feeling of eutierria: a sense of 'oneness' with nature.

Some of the strongest motivations for pantheism are the reasons for rejecting other worldviews. For example, the biggest objection to classical monotheism is the problem of evil and suffering. 'How could an all-loving, all-powerful God allow so many people and animals to suffer so horrendously?' Pantheism side-steps the problem. The God of pantheism isn't beholden to being 'all-powerful' or 'all-loving' – it had no allegiances to scriptures or religious traditions. Therefore, a pantheistic God can fit the evidence as we find it.

Similarly, another colossal challenge for classical monotheism is the problem of divine hiddenness – that is, why the God of classical monotheism doesn't show Himself to His creation more obviously. Why does God hide? Is He shy? On pantheism, what you see is what you get: God, rather than hiding, is on full display, at all times, in all places, to all of the world's creatures.

Pantheism also has an advantage over atheism. Many philosophers have suggested that atheism ignores the fine-tuned nature of the universe and offers a less effective explanation for why there is something (a world) rather than nothing (no world). The cosmic designer, says the pantheist, is the universe itself: an eternally existing God whose conscious intentionally constitutes all of nature. Pantheism explains why the universe exhibits such beauty, order and spirituality. We are already in God's mind. The kingdom of heaven – that is, unity with God – exists here and now.

Everything rather than nothing

Of course, some bizarre consequences may come with believing 'God is everything'. Earlier, I motivated pantheism by using some positive examples of the world's beauty. 'But', the anti-pantheist may protest, 'we can't ignore the more unpleasant, downright horrific parts of the universe.' Not least, your golden retriever's excrement is divine; the gympie-gympie and the rash on your back are a part of God as

> The gympie-gympie, or the 'Queensland stinger', is a stinging nettle found in the rainforests of Malaysia and Australia. Their stings – which can cause months of agonizing pain – can be treated by ingesting tar water.

well. These are minor evils; however, great instances of evil and suffering spread across our planet – natural suffering, for example, such as plagues, viruses, forest fires and the dog-eat-dog laws of nature, to name but a few. What is more, if a malicious species of alien were ever discovered in a neighbouring galaxy, those evil extra-terrestrials would also be part of God. Who knows what evils lurk in the distant corners of our galaxy? Ask yourself this: what *should* the universe look like if a pantheistic God exists? Does it match the small slice of the universe which we inhabit? If you think the answer to the latter question is 'no', then maybe pantheists have their work cut out.

Pantheists may be tempted to say that we exist in a tiny proverbial corner of the universe, which just so happens to have a lot of bad stuff, but that the rest of the universe enjoys overwhelming goodness. That might not convince you. Therefore, I want to suggest a better response: God isn't all-loving and all-powerful. Pantheists aren't obliged to fulfil the description of God as He's portrayed in religious texts. They can bite the bullet. So what? Why should we think that God is all-loving and all-powerful in the first place? Pantheism offers a more effective response to the existence of evil than classical monotheism can provide. On pantheism, the problem of evil is a non-starter. This isn't a shortcoming; it's a virtue. Pantheism offers simple and elegant solutions to the problems of existence. It doesn't need to defend itself; it just needs to adapt.

There may be a bigger problem when it comes to questions of personal identity – such as how conscious entities can keep hold of their individual existences while also being part of God. Opponents have suggested that pantheism is incoherent because it doesn't make sense for you to be you *and* part of God. I think we can overcome this problem. Think of it like this. A nucleus is part of a cell, part of an elbow, part of an arm and part of a body, yet it's still a nucleus. Similarly, I identify as myself (Asha), as a European and as a world-citizen. The same relationship holds for a great number of things. Coral reefs, for example, have individual polyps that constitute pieces of coral: they are both a polyp, part of the coral and part of a coral reef. I can still speak about a single polyp despite it being part of a larger, unified whole. If you can conceive of this type of identity relationship, then it's possible to hold on to our identities while remaining part of God.

Many critics have *panned* the claim (sorry) that the world is God because, as <u>Arthur Schopenhauer</u> scathingly proclaimed, 'it states nothing'.[6] In other words, pantheism is just masquerading as nature-loving atheism; it just gives 'the world' a new name ('God'). Like calling Peter Parker 'Spiderman', the words change, but the objects remain the same. Why might this spell trouble for pantheism? If 'God' is just another name for the universe, then what's the point? Let's just stick to the word we already have! Well, for most pantheists, to call the world 'God' is to say something meaningful about it. Just consider some of the examples we've discussed so far: that the world is divine, a great conscious agent who wills the world's complexity and beauty. That's not another name for the world – especially not Schopenhauer's. 'Pantheism' doesn't say nothing, it tries to describe everything: God, the world and all within it.

> <u>Arthur Schopenhauer</u> (1788–1860) maintained that we can uncover the nature of the world through introspection. When we look inside ourselves, we find 'Will': a sort of consciousness, impulse or drive. Will is the foundation of everything; there is no God, for Will is all that exists. Schopenhauer was also known for his pessimism. Our world, he thought, is the worst of all possible worlds.

Coming home

The idea of humans having a place in the universe as part of nature and God has profound consequences. Most importantly, pantheism gives people a meaningful place in the cosmos. The atheist worldview is hounded for its lack of objective moral values and ultimate purpose. However, if pantheism is true, following the natural order of things is to live according to God's plan. Furthermore, it is a world in which we're no longer alienated. The world isn't just similar to us; it is the *same* as us, as well as our creator. Pantheism is the only philosophy that brings God, the world and all of its creatures into perfect harmony. <u>Joni Mitchell</u> was wrong: we're not just stardust, we're God.[7] Knowing that you are special, divine and an integral part of the universe is nothing to be scoffed at.

> Regardless of whether pantheism is true, philosophers tend to agree that God resides in the music of <u>Joni Mitchell</u>.

This is a universe that ought to be revered and worshipped. The whole world is our temple, and our worship consists of acknowledging the world, appreciating it and giving back to it. I hope that, by seeing the world as God, we might lose some of our anthropocentric tendencies. Everything stands equal in its divinity and, therefore, we should see 'human superiority' for what it is: fiction. We ought to rethink our tendency to use non-human creatures for food, clothing and entertainment to the extent that we do. The same is true for the environment. Pantheism revives our moral responsibilities towards the earth and any other place in the universe to which we might venture. We ought to care for every part of the world: not just humans and non-human animals, but plants, landscapes and the potential extra-terrestrial beings of our futures.

The whole of reality exists within the universe; therefore, pantheism can't offer us eternal salvation. Pantheism doesn't need to align itself with 'religious' views about the afterlife. That might be quite appealing, especially if the thought of living forever in a state of eternal boredom isn't something that floats your boat. I hear the naysayers, 'Well, what's the point then? What's the meaning of life if heaven doesn't exist, if there is no salvation and this universe is all there is?' I answer: the meaning of life is to be good to the ultimate reality that we exist in, to live in harmony with the world, to further our understanding of the cosmos, to embrace the oneness of God and to worship the universe through our actions. What could be more meaningful than that? We,

> In Philip Pullman's *His Dark Materials* (1995–2000), dæmons are physical manifestations of people's inner selves that take the form of non-human animals.

as individual people, aren't going to live forever. Upon death, our physical bodies will decompose, and our atoms will return to the world. As Philip Pullman put it in *His Dark Materials*:

> When you go out of here, all the particles that make you up will loosen and float apart, just like your dæmons did. If you've seen people dying, you know what that looks like. But your dæmons en't just nothing now; they're part of everything. All the atoms that were them, they've gone into the air and the wind and the trees and the earth and all the living things. They'll never vanish. They're just part of everything. You'll drift apart, it's true, but you'll be out in the open, part of everything alive again.[8]

We are part of the world. We always will be.

Afterthoughts

We've come a long way from the God of our opening chapters. Maybe that's where we went wrong; perhaps we just had the wrong idea of God. The 'greatest conceivable being' isn't hiding from us outside of time and space but stands before us in every one of our experiences.

Pantheism doesn't need priests, holy buildings or sacred texts. It can be practised by anyone, anytime, anywhere. This is the ultimate, inclusive religion. It doesn't boast the keys to salvation, demand blinding allegiance or place humans above the rest of creation. Pantheism calls upon us to live in the present and give back to the universe we call home. There is meaning to be discovered in God's plan and morality in the world's order. Yet, there is no afterlife. Instead, our deaths shall sow us back into that which brought us life.

Of course, there are still questions to be answered; the most pressing one being our origins. Is God identical to the Big Bang singularity – the hot, dense entity that contained all of time, space and energy? If pantheism is true, that has to be the case. I wonder how many of us will be satisfied with that answer. If we're disappointed, it's with the realization that this is all there is. Our lives as individual people will someday come to an end.

Yet, there is comfort in belonging. We're already here; there's nowhere else to be. This is our eternal home. We're exactly where we belong.

Questions to consider

1. Can pantheism overcome the afflictions of atheism and theism?
2. If God is identical to the universe, does that explain why there's something rather than nothing?
3. Can we petition the universe to respond to our prayers and desires?
4. Is the world of pantheism more (or less) meaningful than the world of theism?
5. How, if at all, should pantheists worship nature?

Recommended reading

<u>Advanced</u>

Alternative Concepts of God: Essays on the Metaphysics of the Divine, ed. Andrei Buckareff and Yujin Nagasawa (Oxford: Oxford University Press, 2016).

> After centuries of marginalization, alternative concepts of God are finally entering the mainstream. This book, emphasizing pantheistic and panentheistic understanding of God, features fifteen essays from the field's leading scholars. If you enjoyed this chapter, then the essays from Emily Thomas, Yujin Nagasawa and Andrei Buckareff come highly recommended.

Andrei Buckareff, *Pantheism* (Cambridge: Cambridge University Press, 2022).

> This short, technical book is perfect for those who are new to pantheism and are looking to broaden their academic research. Buckareff, one of pantheism's leading authorities, explores what it means to be a 'pantheist', how we should understand God's mind and whether pantheism can accommodate God's personhood.

<u>Intermediate</u>

Ryan Byerly, 'The Awe-some Argument for Pantheism', *European Journal for Philosophy of Religion*, vol. 11, no. 2 (2016): 1–21.

> Whether you think pantheism is awe-ful or awe-some (sorry), you'll enjoy getting your teeth into this essay. Byerly claims that we experience 'awe' when we encounter divine objects. As the universe is the greatest object of awe, he argues that the universe is the most divine object in existence. He ends the article by discussing some objections to pantheism, including versions of (and responses to) the problem of evil.

Asha Lancaster-Thomas, 'The Coherence of Naturalistic Personal Pantheism', *European Journal for Philosophy of Religion*, vol. 12, no. 1 (2020): 75–89.

> Here, Lancaster-Thomas argues that 'physical existence' constitutes a great-making property. Therefore, she says, a God who

is identical to nature is greater (and more worthy of worship) than the timeless, spaceless God of classical monotheism. Furthermore, as well as being the simpler worldview, Asha maintains that pantheism avoids some of the problems faced by traditional theism.

Beginner

Derek Harrison, 'The Gods of Spinoza & Teilhard de Chardin', *Philosophy Now*, 2015, www.philosophynow.org/issues/106/The_Gods_of_Spinoza_and_Teilhard_de_Chardin.

This is a short and accessible essay on the contexts and philosophies of two of pantheism's most important thinkers: Spinoza and Teilhard. As the author explains, Teilhard – writing in the twentieth century – saw Darwinian evolution culminating in a 'physical transformation', in which humanity will ascend to a point of organized, universal consciousness.

Roger Scruton, *Spinoza: A Very Short Introduction* (Oxford: Oxford University Press, 2002).

Baruch Spinoza is history's most important pantheist, and Scruton's book is probably the best introduction to his thought. Spinoza's work defined today's science and philosophy; as a seventeenth-century 'heretic', Spinoza's life is fascinating in its own right.

Notes & Sources

Chapter One

1 'Bill Shankly's Famous "Life And Death" Misquote and What Liverpool Icon Really Meant', *The Mirror*, March 2020, www.mirror.co.uk/sport/football/news/bill-shanklys-famous-life-death-21784583.

2 Plato, *The Republic*, trans. Tom Griffith, ed. G. R. F. Ferrari (Cambridge: Cambridge University Press, 2000), 87–8.

3 Aristotle, *History of Animals: Books I–III*, trans. A. L. Peck (London: Harvard University Press, 1993), 101.

4 George Berkeley, *Siris: A Chain of Philosophical Reflexions and Inquiries Concerning the Virtues of Tar Water, and Divers Other Subjects Connected Together and Arising One from Another* (Dublin: R. Gunnes, 1744), 3.

5 The contributor, Daniel Hill, does not endorse the consumption of tar water. The editor, Jack Symes, recommends it wholeheartedly.

6 Immanuel Kant, *The Metaphysics of Morals*, trans. Mary Gregor, ed. Lara Denis, revised edition (Cambridge: Cambridge University Press, 2017), 190.

7 Friedrich Nietzsche, *The Anti-Christ, Ecce Homo, Twilight of the Idols: An Other Writings*, ed. Aaron Ridley and Judith Norman (Cambridge: Cambridge University Press, 2005), 64, 85–6, 187.

8 Norman Malcolm, *Ludwig Wittgenstein: A Memoir*, 2nd edition (Oxford: Clarendon Press, 2001), 32.

9 Consider Jesus's words in Matthew 12:30, 'Whoever is not with me is against me, and whoever does not gather with me scatters.'

10 Nelson Pike, *God and Timelessness* (Eugene, OR: Wipf and Stock, 2002), 135–6.

11 Blaise Pascal, *Pensées and Other Writings*, trans. Honor Levi, ed. Anthony Levi (Oxford: Oxford University Press, 2008), 152–8.

12 See Jesus's words in Matthew 25:46, 'And they will go away to eternal punishment, but the righteous to eternal life.'

13 FarmVille©, a registered trademark of Zynga games, has no affiliation with Daniel Hill or *Talking about Philosophy*.

14 'The Faith Behind the Famous: Isaac Newton', *Christianity Today*, 1991, www.christianitytoday.com/history/issues/issue-30/faith-behind-famous-isaac-newton.html.

15 Bach's final estate can be viewed online. See 'Specification of the legacy of Johann Sebastian Bach', *JSBach Biografie*, www.jsbach.de/en/node/769.

16 Pascal, *Pensées*, 154.

17 In Pascal's defence, he encourages his readers to wager 'without hesitating' once they've considered his argument. In truth, it was Pascal's friends – who would ask him to calculate the odds on throwing dice – that had the gambling problems . . . Pascal just enabled them.

18 Brian Davies, *Philosophy of Religion: A Guide and Anthology* (Oxford: Oxford University Press, 2000).

Chapter Two

1 Richard Swinburne, *The Coherence of Theism*, 2nd edition (Oxford: Oxford University Press, 2016).
2 Richard Swinburne, *The Existence of God*, 2nd edition (Oxford: Oxford University Press, 2004).
3 Richard Swinburne, *Faith and Reason,* 2nd edition (Oxford: Oxford University Press, 2005).
4 This is not an advertisement. Kellogg's© – or any of their registered trademarks – have not sponsored this book.
5 Swinburne, *Existence of God*, 97–109.
6 Ibid., 293–327.
7 Richard Swinburne, *Providence and the Problem of Evil* (Oxford: Oxford University Press, 1998), 241.
8 Luke 16:19–31.

Chapter Three

1 Mark Twain, *Following the Equator: A Journey Around the World* (Auckland: The Floating Press, 2020), 116.
2 'The Most Influential People in History', *Academic Influence*, 2023, www.academicinfluence.com/people.
3 David Hume, *Dialogues and Natural History of Religion*, ed. John C. A. Gaskin (Oxford: Oxford University Press, 2008), 71.
4 Roger Penrose, 'Time-Asymmetry and Quantum Gravity', in *Quantum Gravity 2: A Second Oxford Symposium*, ed. Chris J. Isham, Roger Penrose and Dennis W. Sciama (Oxford: Clarendon Press, 1981), 249.
5 Qur'an 4:171.
6 Qur'an 4:157–8.
7 Richard Dawkins, *Outgrowing God: A Beginner's Guide* (London: Black Swan, 2020), 39. In this extract, Dawkins approvingly quotes Carl Sagan, who claimed that 'extraordinary claims require extraordinary evidence.'
8 John 3:16.
9 Qur'an 3:30.
10 Qur'an 4:25.
11 Qur'an 4:40.
12 Qur'an 6:140.

Chapter Four

1 Qur'an 4:48.
2 Moses Mendelssohn, *Morning Hours: Lectures on God's Existence*, trans.
   David O. Dahlstrom and Corey Dyck (London: Springer, 2011), 56.
3 The argument in favour of this claim goes like this: If the existence of a
   necessary existent is possible, there is a possible world in which there is a
   necessary existent. But if a necessary existent exists in a possible world, it
   exists in all possible worlds including the actual one.
4 See Jon Hoover, 'A Muslim Conflict over Universal Salvation', in *Alternative
   Salvations: Engaging the Sacred and the Secular*, ed. Hannah Bacon, Wendy
   Dossett and Steve Knowles, (London: Bloomsbury, 2015), 160–71 and
   Marco Demichelis, *Salvation and Hell in Classical Islamic Thought: Can
   Allāh Save Us All?* (London: Bloomsbury, 2018).
5 Avicenna himself defends such a view. See M. E. Marmura, 'Divine
   Omniscience and Future Contingents in Alfarabi and Avicenna', in *Divine
   Omniscience And Omnipotence in Medieval Philosophy: Islamic, Jewish and
   Christian Perspectives*, ed. Tamar Rudavsky (Dordrecht: Springer, 1985), 81–94.
6 Theodore Sider, 'Hell and Vagueness', *Faith and Philosophy* 19, no. 1 (2002):
   58–68.
7 See, among others, Dean Zimmerman, 'The Compatibility of Materialism
   and Survival: the "Falling Elevator" Model', *Faith and Philosophy* 16, no. 2
   (1999): 194–212.
8 See Ahmed Alwishah, 'Ibn Sīnā on Floating Man Arguments', *Journal of
   Islamic Philosophy* 9 (2013): 49–71, and Peter Adamson and Fedor Benevich,
   'The Thought Experimental Method: Avicenna's Flying Man Argument',
   Journal of the American Philosophical Association 4 (2018): 147–64.
9 Zein Ali, 'Some Reflections on William Lane Craig's Critique of Islam', *The
   Heythrop Journal* 60, no. 3 (2019): 397–412.
10 Qur'an 5:171.
11 Some notable philosophers – such as Alexander Pruss – defend amended
   versions of the privation theory, but they represent a disappearing minority.
12 For those looking for another excellent intermediate introductory text, see
   Imran Aijaz, *Islam: A Contemporary Philosophical Investigation* (New York:
   Routledge, 2008).
13 Peter Adamson, *Philosophy in the Islamic World: A Very Short Introduction*
   (Oxford: Oxford University Press, 2015).

Chapter Five

1 This sociological insight is taken from Alvin Plantinga, who – quoting
   John Hick – accepts that it 'may be right'. See Alvin Plantinga, 'Pluralism: A

Defence of Religious Exclusivism', in *The Rationality of Belief & the Plurality of Faith: Essays in Honor of William P. Alston*, ed. Thomas D. Senor (Ithaca, NY: Cornell University Press, 1995), 211.

2 Susan Blackmore, *What Out-of-body Experiences Tell Us About Life, Death and the Mind* (London: Little, Brown, 2017), 1–3.

3 A special thank you to Susan Blackmore for her editorial guidance and contribution to this chapter's introduction.

4 See Ara Norenzayan, *Big Gods: How Religion Transformed Cooperation and Conflict* (Princeton, NJ: Princeton University Press, 2017).

5 For examples, see Pascal Boyer, *Religion Explained: The Evolutionary Origins of Religious Thought* (New York: Basic Books, 2001) and Robin Dunbar, *How Religion Evolved: And Why It Endures* (London: Pelican Books, 2022).

6 Edward O. Wilson, *On Human Nature* (Cambridge, MA: Harvard University Press, 1978), 167.

7 The analogy of vehicles and passengers is borrowed from Richard Dawkins. See Richard Dawkins, *The Selfish Gene* (Oxford: Oxford University Press, 1976), 47.

8 Ibid., 203–15.

9 See Susan Blackmore, *The Meme Machine* (Oxford: Oxford University Press, 1999), 38–42.

10 See Robert Wright, *The Evolution of God: The Origins of Our Beliefs* (London: Little, Brown, 2009).

11 'The Changing Global Religious Landscape', *Pew Research Center*, April 2017, www.pewresearch.org/religion/2017/04/05/the-changing-global -religious-landscape.

12 For an overview, see Christopher Ingraham, 'Charted: The Religions that Make the Most Babies', *The Washington Post*, May 2015, www .washingtonpost.com/news/wonk/wp/2015/05/12/charted-the-religions -that-make-the-most-babies.

13 Patrick J. Weatherhead and Raleigh J. Robertson, 'Offspring Quality and the Polygyny Threshold: "The Sexy Son Hypothesis"', *The American Naturalist* 113, no. 2 (1979): 201–8.

14 See Qur'an 4:34: 'men have been provisioned by Allāh over women . . . if you sense ill-conduct from your women, advise them first, if they persist, do not share their beds, but if they still persist then discipline them gently'.

15 Qur'an 22:19–20.

16 Ayaan Hirsi Ali, *Infidel: My Life* (London: Simon & Schuster, 2007), 80–1.

17 Ibid.

18 Ibid., 239.

19 Ibid., 104.

20 Steije Hofhuis and Maarten Boudry, "'Viral' Hunts? A Cultural Darwinian Analysis of WitchPersecutions', *Cultural Science Journal* 11, no. 1 (2019): 13–29.

21 Gregory S. Paul, 'Cross-National Correlations of Quantifiable Societal Health with Popular Religiosity and Secularism in the Prosperous Democracies', *Journal of Religion & Society* 7 (2005): 1–17.

22 Steve Crabtree, 'Religiosity Highest in World's Poorest Nations', *Gallup*, August 2010, https://news.gallup.com/poll/142727/Religiosity-Highest -World-Poorest-Nations.aspx.

23 *World Happiness Report*, ed. John F. Helliwell, Richard Layard, Jeffrey D. Sachs, Jan-Emmanuel De Neve, Lara B. Aknin and Shun Wang (New York: Sustainable Development Solutions Network, 2022).

24 Ibid., 17–19.

25 In the United States, *God Is Not Great* was published with the subtitle '*How Religion Poisons Everything*' (New York: Twelve Books, 2007).

Chapter Six

1 Charles Darwin, *On the Origin of Species by Means of Natural Selection* (London: John Murray, 1859).

2 Dawkins, *The Selfish Gene*.

3 Richard Dawkins, *The Blind Watchmaker: Why the Evidence of Evolution Reveals a Universe Without Design* (London: Penguin Books, 1986).

4 Richard Dawkins, *The God Delusion* (London: Transworld, 2006).

5 'World Thinkers 2013', *Prospect Magazine*, April 2013, www .prospectmagazine.co.uk/magazine/world-thinkers-2013.

6 Bertrand Russell, *Why I Am Not a Christian: And Other Essays on Religion and Related Subjects* (London: Routledge, 2004), 1–19, 18.

7 Bertrand Russell, *What I Believe* (London: Routledge, 2013).

8 Dawkins, *God Delusion*, 50–1.

9 *C. G. Jung Speak: Interviews and Encounters*, ed. R. F. C. Hull (Princeton, NJ: Princeton University Press, 1977), 428.

10 William Paley, *Natural Theology: Or Evidence of the Existence and Attributes of the Deity, Collected from the Appearances of Nature*, ed. Matthew D. Eddy and David Knight (Oxford: Oxford University Press, 2008), 16, 172.

11 Darwin, *Origin of Species*, 186.

12 Dawkins, *Blind Watchmaker*, 5–6.

13 Lawrence Krauss, *A Universe from Nothing: Why There Is Something Rather than Nothing* (New York: Simon & Schuster, 2012), 176.

14 Paley, *Natural Theology*, 199.

15 Ibid., 238.

16 *The Correspondence of Charles Darwin: Volume 8*, ed. Frederick Burkhardt (Cambridge: Cambridge University, 1993), 224.

17 Ann Coulter, *Godless: The Church of Liberalism* (New York: Crown Forum, 2006), 172.

Chapter Seven

1 Formerly President of the British Society for the Philosophy of Religion, Yujin is currently the Editor of the leading international journal *Religious Studies*, Co-director of the Birmingham Centre for Philosophy of Religion and Project Lead of the £2.15 million research initiative the Global Philosophy of Religion Project.
2 Richard Dawkins, *An Appetite for Wonder: The Making of a Scientist* (London: Black Swan, 2014), 3.
3 Richard Dawkins, 'Atheism is the New Fundamentalism', *Intelligence Squared*, November 2009, https://youtu.be/lheDgyaItOA, 1:50–2:35.
4 Albert Camus, *The Myth of Sisyphus* (London: Penguin Books, 2005), 119.
5 William Lane Craig, *Reasonable Faith: Christian Truth and Apologetics*, 3rd edition (Wheaton, IL: Crossway Books, 2008), 65–92.
6 This is not an advertisement. Terry's Chocolate Orange© have not responded to several invitations to be affiliated with this book.
7 Dominic D. P. Johnson and James H. Fowler, 'The Evolution of Overconfidence', *Nature* 477, no. 7364 (2011): 317–20.
8 David Benatar, 'Better Never to Have Been: The Harm of Coming into Existence', *Mind* 117, no. 467 (2008): 674–7.

Chapter Eight

1 Saint Augustine, *Confessions*, trans. Henry Chadwick (Oxford: Oxford University Press, 2008), 31. (My emphasis.)
2 Edward Madden and Peter Hare, *Evil and the Concept of God* (Springfield, IL: Charles C. Thomas, 1968), 32–4.
3 Ibid., 34.
4 Steven Cahn, 'Cacodaemony', *Analysis* 37, no. 2 (1977): 69–73.
5 Christopher New, 'Antitheism: A Reflection', *Ratio* 6, no. 1 (1993): 36–43.
6 For numerous examples, see the *Skeptical Inquirer* magazine.
7 See Asha Lancaster-Thomas, 'The Evil-God Challenge Part II: Objections and Responses', *Philosophy Compass* 13, no. 8 (2018): 1–10.

Chapter Nine

1 Albert Einstein, 'Einstein Believes in Spinoza's "God"', *New York Times*, April 1929, www.nytimes.com/1929/04/25/archives/einstein-believes-in-spinozas-god-scientist-defines-his-faith-in.html.
2 Robert Frost, *Robert Frost's Poems* (New York: St. Martin's, 2002), 163.

3   Carol Pipes, 'ACP: More Churches Reported; Baptisms Decline', *Baptist Press*, June 2016, www.baptistpress.com/resource-library/news/acp-more-churches -reported-baptisms-decline.

4   Thomas Hobbes, *Leviathan*, ed. Christopher Brooke (London: Penguin Books, 2017), 103–5.

Chapter Ten

1   Karl Marx, *Early Writings*, ed. Joseph O'Malley and Richard A. Davis (Cambridge: Cambridge University Press, 1994), 57.

2   Alvin Plantinga, 'Advice to Christian philosophers', *Faith and Philosophy* 1, no. 3 (1984): 256–64.

3   John Cottingham, 'Transcending Science: Humane Models of Religious Understanding', in *New Models of Religious Understanding*, ed. Fiona Ellis (Oxford: Oxford University Press, 2018), 24.

4   See Michael Behe, *Darwin's Black Box: The Biochemical Challenge to Evolution* (New York: Free Press, 1996). Here, Behe tries to construct such an argument from irreducible complexity. However, the argument's central premise – that there do exist irreducibly complex natural phenomena that cannot be explained within the framework of Darwinian evolutionary theory – is doubted by the vast majority of natural scientists. As a consequence, the argument has not received much philosophical attention.

5   Dietrich Bonhoeffer, *Letters and Papers from Prison*, ed. Eberhard Bethge (London: SMC Press, 2017), 111.

6   Bonhoeffer lived a fascinating life. It's worth checking out a good biography, such as Eric Metaxas, *Bonhoeffer: Pastor, Martyr, Prophet, Spy* (Nashville, TN: Thomas Nelson, 2011).

7   Ariela Keysar and Juhem Navarro-Rivera, 'A World of Atheism: Global Demographics', in *The Oxford Handbook of Atheism*, ed. Stephen Bullivant and Michael Ruse (Oxford: Oxford University Press, 2013), 553.

8   Ibid., 571.

9   See Scott Atran and Ara Norenzayan, 'Religion's Evolutionary Landscape: Counterintuition, Commitment, Compassion, Communion', *Behavioral and Brain Sciences* 27, no. 6 (2004): 713–30 and Dominic Johnson and Jesse Bering, 'Hand of God, Mind of Man: Punishment and Cognition in the Evolution of Cooperation', *Evolutionary Psychology* 4 (2006): 219–33.

10 See Michael J. Murray, 'Scientific Explanations of Religion and the Justification of Religious Belief', in *The Believing Primate: Scientific, Philosophical, and Theological Reflections on the Origins of Religion*, ed. Jeffrey Schloss and Michael J. Murray (Oxford: Oxford University Press, 2009), 168–78.

11 Bertrand Russell, *Mysticism and Logic: And Other Essays* (London: George Allen & Unwin Ltd, 1917), 1.

Chapter Eleven

1   *The Rig Veda*, trans. Wendy Doniger (London: Penguin Books, 1975), 25.
2   See Thomas Aquinas, *Compendium of Theology*, trans. Richard J. Regan (Oxford: Oxford University Press, 2009), 53–4.
3   *Upaniṣads*, trans. Patrick Olivelle (Oxford: Oxford University Press, 1996), 154–5.
4   '1980s: A Health Crisis, And Authorial Success', *Hawking.org*, www.hawking .org.uk/biography.
5   *The Bhagavad Gita*, trans. Gavin Flood and Charles Martin (London: W. W. Norton & Company, 2013), 89–100.
6   Ibid., 15.
7   Taylor Swift, 'Karma', *Midnights* (Republic Records, 2022).
8   Klaus K. Klostermaier, *Hinduism: A Short History* (Oxford: Oneworld Publications, 2000).

Chapter Twelve

1   William Wordsworth, *Selected Poems: William Wordsworth* (London: Macmillan, 2004), 48.
2   Guy Adams, '"Pantheist" Lincoln Would Be Unelectable Today', *Independent*, April 2011, www.independent.co.uk/news/world/americas/pantheist-lincoln -would-be-unelectable-today-2269024.
3   Philip Goff, 'Galileo's Error', in *Philosophers on Consciousness: Talking about the Mind*, ed. Jack Symes (London: Bloomsbury, 2022), 130–1.
4   Walt Whitman, *Song of Myself* (London: Penguin Books, 2015), 170.
5   Ronald W. Knapp, 'Pantheism', in *The Routledge Encyclopedia of Walt Whitman*, ed. J. R. Le Master and Donald D. Kummings (New York: Garland Publishing, 1998), 504.
6   Arthur Schopenhauer, *Parerga and Paralipomena*, vol. 2, trans. E. F. J. Payne (Oxford: Oxford University Press, 2000), 99.
7   Joni Mitchell, 'Woodstock', *Ladies of the Canyon* (Warner Records, 1970).
8   Philip Pullman, *The Amber Spyglass* (New York: Alfred A. Knopf, 2000), 319.

Index

Note Page numbers followed by "n" refer to notes.

optimism 100
optimists 100
original sin 107–8
origin of life 78
'oscillating models' of universe 32
Otto, R. 167
outdated arguments 122–5
out-of-body experience 61

pain 131–2
Paley, W. 84
   Natural Theology 80
Pandora's box 111
Pannenberg, W. 39
pantheism 37, 163–72
   collective 165
   distributive 165
Pascal, B. 6–9, 87, 175 n. 17
   'Pascal's wager' 6–9
Paul, G. 72
Penrose, Sir R. 34
perfect freedom 18
pessimism 129–32
philosophy
   definition of 46
   game 122
   nature of 78
   of religion 47, 159
   and science, relationship
      between 12, 46, 78
physicalism 166
Pike, N.
   God and Timelessness 4
Pinker, S.
   Better Angels of Our Nature,
      The 131
   Enlightenment Now 131
Plantinga, A. 31–2, 113, 120–1,
      124, 138
Plato 2, 53, 78, 136
'play' (*līlā*) 155
Plotinus 136
polytheism 48
power to sin 15

precognitive dreams 62
prejudice 56
Presley, E. 86
Princess Diana 86
privation theory of evil 53, 57
problem of good 105
'proof of the sincere' 49
Prophet Muhammad 48
   flight to heaven 86
Protestantism 128
Pruss, A. 177 n. 11
psychokinesis 62
Pullman, P.
   His Dark Materials 171

quantum theory 83
questions of God 47
Qur'an 39–41, 52, 55, 56
   afterlife 54
   infidel 71
   memeplex, structure of 69

racial equality 68
Radha 154
random mutation 139
rationality of theism 135–45
reasonable faith 29–42
rebirth, cycle of 157
'red in tooth and claw' 84
reductios 124
Reformation 128
reformed epistemology 120–2
reincarnation 157
religious experience 21
   supernatural explanations
      of 21–2
religious pluralism 30
replicator 65
reverse-theodicies 107
ṛta 152–3
Russell, B. 79
   History of Western Philosophy,
      A 149
   'Mysticism and Logic' 142–3